Surviving and Thriving

EVELYN SINCLAIR

Contents

1	From Scotland to Nigeria	7
2	Life in Oji River	17
3	Cross-cultural Issues	23
4	A Very Different Teaching Experience	29
5	Christmas and Bombs	35
6	Evacuate from Oji to Enugu to Akeme - Uno	45
7	Biafra Declares Independence	55
8	A War-time Birth	65
9	I Return to Scotland with Ngozi	71
10	Our Time in Glasgow	89
11	A Reluctant Return to Nigeria	107
12	Leaving Nigeria - AGAIN	117
13	Welcome back to Scotland	125
14	Resolving our Routines	135
15	A Final Adventure	139
	Epilogue	147

Surviving and Thriving

Chapter One

From Scotland to Nigeria

Take a young Scots woman with a rebellious attitude, move her to an African country where an internal civil war occurs and expect trouble.

Did I realise the consequences of my rebellious attitude? There is no way I could possibly have foreseen the unbelievable nightmares that would follow my decision. My distinctive and complex personality was undoubtedly influenced by my early life experiences.

My family lives in Sandbank on the shores of the Holy Loch. I don't know why it's so-called but we're told an Irish monk in the sixth century sailed in his coracle across the Irish Sea, up the Firth of Clyde and into this small loch where he founded a monastery, hence the name "Holy Loch". Sandbank, on the southern shore of the loch, is a small rural community of around 200 inhabitants, and it is here that I grew up, attending the local church with my parents and brothers. Finding my identity among three brothers felt problematic. I definitely did not want to join them in their various escapades and this made me feel "different". I had to learn to stand up for myself, to think independently, do my own thing and sometimes to be a little secretive about what I might be thinking or doing, but not saying.

As I was a bright teenager, the advice to my working-class parents from "those who know best" was that I should be trained as a teacher and so, innocent and seventeen years old I set off to Glasgow University. Here I meet Sennen, a handsome, intelligent, beguiling Nigerian. He is studying mechanical engineering and I am captivated by the stories of his homeland. We spend most of our free time together; I am completely obsessed with this relationship and the inherent potential for foreign travel and adventure which it offers.

Regular visits back to Sandbank find me enthusing to my parents about my geography and geology classes. There are also university clubs to be mentioned and it is here that dissension begins to appear.

"I have joined a number of clubs to gain new skills and experiences. It's all so exciting." I tell my parents.

"What kind of clubs are there and what are they all about?"

"Well, there's the Christian Union, I knew you'd want me to join that. We are currently studying a series on Paul's journeys and I find this really interesting. Reading and discussing his travels and adventures are a challenge to us all in respect to what God is calling each of *us* to do. Also hearing about missionaries such as Gladys Aylward who served in China, and Mary Slessor who worked in Nigeria excited my interest in evangelism linked to foreign travel. Then there's the judo club, and during one meeting I broke my partner's collarbone, but it wasn't really my fault as she didn't fall the proper way. I wasn't blamed for the accident, and I know she's fine now. I'm also learning to fence, and once when I lunged at my partner, my trousers split up the back seam and everyone had a good laugh at me."

I hesitate before continuing. *How will the next bit of information be received?*

"Being a geography student I wondered about the International Society, so I went along there too. It's really interesting—students from all around the world—and I am now friendly with a Nigerian who is studying engineering, the same course as Campbell (my older brother). He is a Christian and knows about Mary Slessor's work among his people."

A look passes between my parents, but all I hear is "Mmm," and the tone does not sound very encouraging.

Has Campbell been talking to them about my friend Sennen?

Sennen is extremely courteous at the Society meetings, seeming to pay attention mainly to me, and I am flattered and completely smitten. No young man has ever shown me this kind of consideration before, and certainly not my brothers. We begin spending more and more of our free time together. He speaks excitedly to me about the recent independence (1960) of his homeland, and I am entranced by the stories he shares with me of music, culture, dance, native medicines, festivals, wildlife, fruits, traditional foods and so many more things. This is my geographical studies being turned into reality.

The only downside to our developing friendship is that when walking out together and holding hands in public, we are often subjected to varying degrees of racial abuse. I am taken aback by the things that teenagers shout at us, and the unconcealed displeasure of passing adults. No matter how frequently we experience these incidents—and there are many—we manage it by refusing to react, considering it to be ignorance and stupidity on the part of those trying to bully, alienate or intimidate us.

Time passes; I graduate and continue on my planned course, attending the local teacher training college and combining the teaching certificate studies with a Diploma in Education course back at the University. Sennen is now completing the fourth year of his studies and graduates in tandem with the completion of my training.

I want Sennen to visit Sandbank, meet my parents and for them to like him. I am utterly shocked when they refuse to see him. *Is this a display of racism on their part, or do they fear facing up to potential prejudices from neighbours and friends?*

"You must stop all this nonsense and find other friends." I am instructed, during a home visit. "You will be throwing away all your education and there is no future for you in this relationship."

"It's not like that, Dad. We have already been talking about going back together to Nigeria. Sennen has a high ranking position waiting for him with the electricity corporation, so we will be quite well off, and I can also teach out there. There's no real need to worry about us."

"Know now that we will not attend any wedding you may be planning, and you will be on your own if you pursue these disastrous plans."

"But Dad, I am your only daughter; you can't be so cruel about my intentions. Please!"

"Your plans for your life, as you describe them, are a fantasy. Get real! And just remember what your mother and I have said."

How can they be so blinkered and hurtful without even having met the man I love?

I am determined to follow through on my own decision to marry and emigrate. My rebellion over this results in my parents refusing to attend our wedding. However, we go ahead and are married in the University Chapel among our close friends, and shortly afterward set off for Nigeria. This creates a major family upset, and I hear nothing from my parents, although I have tried to keep them informed and involved. *Do they not realise how independent and obstinate I have been all my life?* The situation saddens me, but for better or for worse I have made my decision.

Surviving and Thriving

The time approaches for us to make the journey. Friends have given us wedding presents which are unbreakable, in the knowledge that we will be making the long trip by sea. Apart from my bridesmaid's traditional gift of a tea set, most guests have presented us with table linen, bed linen, towels and kitchen essentials. We are therefore able to pack all our belongings into trunks with little fear of breakages, and we set off on our adventure. My collection of fossils garnered during university excursions also comes with us. We spend two idyllic weeks at sea. I am interested to observe that many of the other passengers are Africans, and I later discover that like Sennen, they have been studying in the UK and are now as excited as we are to be returning to their various homelands in West Africa. The voyage lasts two weeks. Cruising like this is, for me, a new and seemingly very exotic style of travel, with all our needs being met and no practical demands being made on my time. I don't even think about the fact that tickets have been paid for, presumably by Sennen. There are several restaurants on board the ship, serving both European and African cuisine. We explore the variety of available eating places, some formal and others completely informal. The menus on offer provide me with the opportunity to sample a number of African dishes. I notice that many of these dishes are cooked using chilli pepper, and most are based on rice.

As expected, the crossing of the Bay of Biscay is somewhat rough, but thereafter the voyage continues very smoothly. We pass our time lounging in deck chairs, and when feeling a bit more energetic we can choose the swimming pool or play one of the many deck games which are available.

The route along the west coast of Africa is punctuated by docking firstly at Dakar, then Freetown, followed by Abidjan and Accra, before finally berthing in Lagos. While the ship is in port I begin to experience the humid, tropical heat and realise that I need to protect my pale skin from this searing, sweltering, burning sun. As we disembark I'm trembling with excitement (or is it with apprehension?) about the reality of this unknown world to which I am now committed.

Lagos lies some 500 miles west of our final destination, but we will later complete our journey by road. After sorting out our luggage and hotel overnight accommodation, we venture into town for a short exploration. The streets in Lagos are full of traders selling all kinds of goods from their small stalls. On show are clay cooking pots, bales of cloth in vibrant colours and displaying exotic designs, local vegetables which I have yet to learn to name and to cook, herbal medicines and other strange items—at least to my eyes. There are also market stalls with a variety of traditionally cooked food on offer, but it is the fruit stalls which catch my attention. Here, I am attracted by the fresh scents drifting from the stalls, and I find an abundance of oranges, bananas, mangoes, lemons, kiwi fruit and avocados on sale for just one penny each. *How can they be so cheap?* So I have my first experience of fresh street food: I opt for something familiar—an orange—which the stall holder cuts in half and hands to me. The traditional way to eat it is to suck out the flesh and the juice, extracting every last bit of the fruit by turning the skin completely inside out, and then casually disposing of the skins in the gutter! This explains the prevalence of dried up abandoned fruit skins I had noticed without comprehending what they actually were. The fruit is so deliciously sweet and juicy, more so than any orange I have previously tasted.

When Sennen is able finally to move me on from here, we walk to the beach. Tantalising new visual prospects await me: miles of silver sand, waves gently lapping the shoreline of the lagoon, palm trees softly swaying in a cooling breeze, and I am excited to see real coconuts actually growing near the tops of trees. Sennen points to various trees:

"Can you see the bunches of nuts at the top of these other trees?" he asks, pointing, and his arm is around me as he continues, "These are palm oil trees, and they are an important economic resource to Nigeria on account of the huge variety of products which make use of palm oil."

"Oh yes, now I see them. What can they be used for?"

"Well for starters, when we cook with oil it is always with palm oil from these nuts. The oil also goes into margarine, crisps, some cheeses, soaps, shampoos and is even being investigated as a possible biofuel."

This is yet another indication of the many more surprises awaiting me. As we stroll on, there are natural exotic floral displays, plants which I do not recognise, but I hope later to establish their names. So much excitement within a few hours of setting foot in my new homeland! This is turning out to be an even more thrilling adventure that I had imagined, and I am totally enthralled. Everything is even more mesmerising. I feel so positive and fortunate to be here enjoying all these tropical delights. Even the temperature which was so uncomfortable when we first disembarked is being moderated by the breeze from the ocean.

We spend our first night here in Lagos. The hotel we use is quite luxurious and not at all what I was expecting. Again my expectations are being far surpassed. The following day we go shopping. Not for food or for clothes, but for a car - a company car to which Sennen is entitled. Thus far in my life, I have never known of such business opportunities or personal wealth which seems now to be my lot. I am beginning to enjoy it immensely, but I definitely feel like the proverbial innocent abroad.

If my parents could only see me now, they would stop worrying and be happy for me.

Chapter Two

Life in Oji River

The following morning we set off in our newly purchased Peugeot 404 and drive the 500 miles east, on an excellent two-lane highway bordered by jungle. Again I am astounded, this time by the quality of the roads. They may be lacking lay-bys and road markings, but they are definitely very smooth, with no evidence of potholes. There is not much to see in the way of scenery as we travel. The trees edging the road are pretty tall and dense. I am seeing "jungle" in reality for the first time and it is denser than any forest I have ever seen back home in Scotland. Travelling onwards I recognise banana trees at the roadside, laden with ripening fruit, and I spot other trees bearing various fruits. There seems to be such a huge variety, all fighting for space and sunlight, many with their fruits hanging in bunches from the branches. We eventually pass through Benin City, the capital of the mid-west state, and soon after, we drive across the River Niger. This is the main bridging point on the river and takes us into the eastern state, where later that evening we arrive at our new home in the small rural settlement of Oji River. We are 6° north of the equator, so I realise that I will be experiencing very different "seasons" and temperatures compared to back home.

The tiny village of Oji River is well known for two reasons. Firstly, the largest electricity power station in the eastern state is situated here. Secondly, there is also a leprosy rehabilitation centre based here, which is overseen by missionaries from the Plymouth Brethren. The local church is close by and this is where we will be worshipping. The power station is where Sennen will be working, as Nigeria's first indigenous senior manager. It is built on the banks of the River Oji which provides the water to the cooling system for the turbines.

With Sennen's posting comes a beautiful modern two-storey home with four bedrooms, full air-conditioning, terrazzo flooring and all mod cons included. It is sited in an exclusive location, with a small number of neighbouring bungalows for the expatriate staff—senior employees at the power station. These homes are all built on a slightly higher part of the land, a mile from the power station, and with no other immediate neighbours. Piped water comes from an underground source, so unlike the nearby villagers, we have the "luxury" of running water and associated facilities. All the homes here have plenty of green space, and large gardens bordered by the jungle where it is sometimes possible to hear monkeys chattering, cicadas chirping and birds singing. Within the gardens, we are visited by snakes, flies and other insects including mosquitoes and a variety of ants: flying ants which I later learn to cook and eat, and soldier ants which I quickly learn to avoid at all costs! It is fascinating to watch a column of soldier ants traverse the grass—an endless column about an inch wide, comprised of thousands of these tiny creatures who take no prisoners "en route". I'm told that when they come to a stream they simply keep on marching, walking on top of those which have entered the water just ahead of them. One of our neighbours keeps a few hens in his garden supplying eggs and fresh meat, but after the soldier ants cross his garden one evening they leave only bare bones and feathers to be found in the morning. Our homes all have protective mesh on the windows which serves as a deterrent from both the soldier ants and the mosquitoes, meaning we enjoy the freedom of sleeping without the use of protective nets around our beds. This is high end living indeed.

Crocodiles use the river by the power station, or so I'm told, and there are obstructions to prevent them from being drawn into the cooling system. I am intrigued by the idea of crocodiles close by, but I am never fortunate enough to see any.

How I love to step out of the house and pick fresh guavas from the garden, which taste tantalisingly similar to my memory of savouring strawberries and cream. I can also smell the beautiful bougainvillea flowers, pick some to adorn the house, or collect ripe mangoes from the driveway for supper. Sometimes, to escape the heat, I use our private outdoor swimming pool, or just laze on the shaded veranda of the house and count my many, many blessings. We have a gardener who looks after the surrounding areas of all the homes, and another person who keeps the swimming pool clean and refreshed. All these workmen are employed by and paid for by the ECN—Electricity Corporation of Nigeria.

Life seems that it just cannot get any better. So I decided to develop a small garden plot and grow some yams—being the staple equivalent of potatoes in the UK. Most expatriates and senior government employees recruit trained house-boys who speak good English and cook traditional European food. Sennen has decided to do things differently. By offering a housemaid's position to an un-schooled young village girl, Charity, he is offering her a chance to improve herself in many ways. She has the opportunity to learn good English, and as a by-product, I may learn to speak some Igbo. That's a win/win formula. I can also potentially teach her to bake, sew clothing and perhaps also to knit—all skills which can later help her to secure an independent lifestyle. Her accommodation is in an outhouse comprising several small individual rooms adjacent to our house, and we equip one of the rooms with a sleeping mat and a cupboard for her personal belongings.

I'm a keen gardener—courtesy of my parents and a rural upbringing—so Charity and I dig a patch of ground, and create some mounds where we plant a few yams. In another area, we plant cassava, beans, and okra. As the yams grow, their tendrils require staking, so I twist them up around some canes. The next day they have unwound themselves and are back on the ground. So I twist them up the canes again. Down they come again! Charity laughs so much she can barely talk. Although she is much younger than me, she is obviously wiser in the local farming ways, and she points out that the tendrils will only grow in an anti-clockwise direction, which is definitely not how I am trying to train them. With the yam problem resolved we are now underway and are going to be self-sufficient in carbs and vegetables. We plant tomatoes, pumpkins, a leafy green vegetable, and okra. I find this quite fulfilling and think back to our family garden in Scotland where my father grew potatoes, leeks, onions, beans, and soft fruits.

Surviving and Thriving

Chapter Three

Cross-cultural Issues

One thing I have not appreciated until now is that while in Scotland, Sennen's behaviour was apparently much westernised, but on returning to his homeland he resumes a more cultural identity and that involves a change in behaviour towards me. This creates confusing expectations for me in my role as an Igbo wife. Initially being viewed with huge respect as a white educated wife with additional talents, I soon go from being the "trophy" wife to being a despised "barren" wife. An immediate pregnancy following marriage is an Igbo expectation and I am, therefore, a huge disappointment and embarrassment to Sennen and his family. *Is this the bed I have made for myself, in rebelling against my parents?* My reaction is to revert to silence laced with a measure of passive aggression—reminiscent of sibling fights and survival—and so Sennen and I have fewer meaningful discussions about anything as the days go by, and still, I do not conceive.

One evening he returns from work and we have a heated exchange.

"That's NOT a GIFT, it's a BRIBE!" he explodes.

"It's not for you. It was a present for ME!"

"Listen to what I am telling you, and understand that any so-called gift from any of my employees is a bribe, and must not be accepted. Just remember that!"

Tears jump to my eyes and my heart is thumping. Our first serious row! Just an hour previously I had accepted a freshly caught fish from one of his men on the doorstep, and this is the thanks I am getting. I fear I have much to learn about living in a West African culture. I'm beginning to realise the implications of a strongly patriarchal society, and I don't think I can, nor will I, meekly comply with this kind of requirement, husband or no husband. I need to find a way to circumvent such requests while remaining true to myself. Our current altercation means I must learn how to decline subsequent "gifts" without causing offence. Later, offerings of local beer arrive on a fairly regular footing, but I feel well able to decline these on the basis that we are both teetotal, and I don't even report these incidents to Sennen.

However, some months later a different kind of gift elicits a totally different response both from me and from Sennen. I respond to a knock at the door and on the doorstep is a workman with a goat—a real live bleating goat on a rope. *This is interesting.* I'm not quick enough to come up with a reasonable excuse to decline **this** particular gift. I also do not want to offend but want to know more, and so I make my own decision and resolve that I **will** accept the offering. At the same time, I feel extremely apprehensive and wary about how my husband will react when he finds out what I have just done, as I am blatantly disobeying his instructions. I thank the man, take the goat and lead it into the thick trees just beyond the boundary of our garden and tie it to a papaya (pawpaw) tree, where it can graze while being in the shade. When Sennen returns home in the evening, I delay and delay before casually reporting what I have done. To my utter surprise and amazement, when I eventually confess, his reaction could not be more different and so much calmer when compared to what had happened over the fresh fish; although the fish was fresh it was already dead, unlike the goat.

"Well," he says, "this presents a great opportunity for you to host your first traditional feast. All you need to do is fatten up the goat, slaughter it, cook it and then we will call the worker and invite him and his family to come and share in our feast. We will all enjoy the meal—goat is a special delicacy—and I will arrange for some traditional music and dancing."

"Did you just say slaughter?" I respond. "I don't know the first thing about slaughtering an animal. A chicken maybe, but a goat, NOOOOOO. No way."

"Oh well," is the straightforward reply, "Charity will

show you how to do it." and that seems to be that.

The goat continues to spend his days in the shade of the forest, and spend the nights secured in one of the rooms of the outhouse. During the next few weeks, I do little to ensure the welfare of this animal. I am now much more concerned—and constantly worrying about—how I can slaughter the animal; prepare and cook the meat. Sometime later, our goat is looking really well fed and is ready for the chop. The time for the feast is fast approaching when one day Charity runs into the house, all sweaty and panicky, looking for me. She brings what, for me, is exciting and very welcome news:

"Madam, oh Madam I can't find our goat. This morning I tie him in the forest, and I tie him well. When I go to check if he is grazing, he isn't there and his rope is also gone. Madam, please, please, don't punish me."

My stomach contracts, I shake with suppressed laughter, but I manage to maintain a straight face. This is the best news I can possibly have. No goat means no slaughtering and no preparation or cooking for our feast. I shall miss the music and dancing but I can't express my feelings of delight and total relief at this turn of events. Sennen will not be at all happy about it, but if the goat has been stolen, as appears to be the case, there is nothing he can do about it, and we are unlikely to solve the mystery or catch the thief.

"Charity, have you looked around in the forest and searched for the goat?"

"Yes, Madam. I have searched very, very far and I don't see him. Also, I check for another animal that might eat him, and I don't see that either."

"Well, there is nothing more we can do. Just continue with your duties in the house, and don't worry about it. No one is going to punish you."

Meanwhile, I'm thinking: *This is really good news and brings a happy ending to all the uncertainties around my future cultural responsibilities for a feast. This time I feel as if I have the victory.*

Several months of this easy undemanding lifestyle begins to dull on me in certain aspects. Being a trained teacher I recognise that it is my unemployed status which is irking me. I am missing the challenges of the classroom, and I mention this in passing to Sennen, never thinking that he would want a "working wife", given his status in the community. However, he returns one evening and unexpectedly announces:

"I have found you a teaching job."

"Oh. Where? How come? Tell me more about this." *I register that this decision has been finalised before consulting with me.*

"Well, there is a mission school at Achi, about ten miles from here. I have spoken with the head teacher and he would be delighted to have you as his first English trained white teacher." He explains, "English is not the boys' first language, but it is the language used in the classroom, so you would be a real bonus in that respect."

"Boys?"

"It's a boys' secondary level residential school, run by the Anglican Mission, CMS. The post is in line with your qualifications, but you'll need your own transport to get there on a daily basis."

Sennen then goes about finding transport, and soon afterwards he procures a Honda motorbike for me. I'm uncertain whether my British driving license covers me for this, but after investigating I discover that there are no Nigerian restrictions I need to be concerned about, and I quickly become competent riding and controlling my new vehicle. No rules, no helmet, I'm on my way.

Chapter Four

A Very Different Teaching Experience

Thus begins a very interesting, satisfying and sometimes humorous episode in my life. The "boys" are aged between sixteen and twenty-nine—I am twenty-three. It is a boarding school, and the fees of most students are being paid by combined financial contributions from extended family members. Families operate this way to create the educational opportunity for a bright youngster which may prove to be a pathway out of poverty for the family.

Frequently as I travel to school, I find myself scattering the proverbial "chickens crossing the road". Free-ranging hens strut out from the edges of the bush and then scatter in panic at the noise from my motorbike. This is one of many hazards I have to negotiate. Another is that the path from the road into the school grounds is composed of soft sand, across which I must weave my precarious final hundred yards to my classroom.

I find the students to be very respectful, and on my entering the classroom the regular pattern is that they all rise and await my greeting, "Good morning boys," to which they respond "Good morning Madam." The local language is tonal with a single word having various unrelated meanings, dependent on where the inflections are placed, so the students are listening very attentively to my voice. Initially, I do not recognise how closely they are using a Scottish accent when greeting me. A few months later, however, an American Peace Corps volunteer joins the staff. One morning when my class is settled and quiet, I hear the young American man entering the adjoining classroom. His greeting is the standard "Good morning boys." The boys respond routinely but mimic his strong Texan accent. This arouses my curiosity, and so I listen much more thoughtfully to what is being said to me! That typical rolling of the Scottish "rrrr"; "Good morrrrning madam" is quite distinct as I listen more closely to the way I am being greeted. The tonality of the Igbo language is causing the boys to copy as closely as possible the way they hear English being spoken. I still smile when I remember this, and think of the potential for confusion, had there been several more English accents around in the school.

One other cultural curiosity for the boys is that I am left-handed. In Nigeria, the left hand is traditionally seen as the dirty hand (following toilet visits), and so it is never used in an interactive situation, such as in the offering, receiving or exchanging of an item, be it money, gifts, or food etc. It is thus always totally unacceptable to use one's left hand. When shopping in the market I am getting used to offering my money to the trader only with my right hand and receiving my change back, again, only into my right hand. For me this is awkward, but custom prevails and I must accept that. In addition, if an infant shows a preference for their left hand to take something, its hand is sharply and repeatedly slapped down, so I never come across a left-handed pupil. The blackboard is a length of plywood, painted black and attached to the back wall of the room. As I start writing at the left-hand end of this blackboard I naturally use my left hand. I hear a gasp from the students. I accept this as some kind of disapproval, but when I reach the middle of the blackboard, I simply transfer the chalk to my right hand and continue writing across the board to the other end. Now they are really confused and don't quite know what to make of me. However, they do eventually get used to seeing me operate in this way and are able finally, to see the funny side of my method of writing on their loooong blackboard.

I love teaching in this environment where there are no classroom disturbances. The students are all very aware of the responsibility they carry on behalf of their families and are so keen to learn and be at their best. If there is a minor disturbance the boys will deal with it themselves in the playground, so on the whole, the classroom experience for me is calm and productive.

I begin by teaching geography, which is my main subject.

I have no visual aids to work with, so I make my own. I build mountains from layers of cardboard to demonstrate contour lines in mapping, and I build a globe from two intersecting circles with which I can demonstrate the tilt of the earth. With my globe, I help the boys to understand why Nigerian days are all twelve hours of daylight and twelve hours of darkness, while Scotland has long summer days and long winter nights. However, sometime later I am asked to take on some English literature teaching with the senior boys. I agree, and then the anomalies begin to present themselves. We don't study "Things Fall Apart" or "Arrow of God" by Chinua Achebe, an Igbo author. Oh no. We are studying "Far from the Madding Crowd" by Thomas Hardy; things like snow and hay, as well as English lifestyles, are completely foreign concepts to the students. How do you describe snow to boys living in a tropical zone? My best suggestion is, "Try scraping out the frost from a fridge, toss it into the air, and as it falls to the ground think about snow!"

I tell them about snowball fights, building snowmen, sledging, skating, and skiing. They show a lot of interest in all these things but are quite sure they would not like to live in such a cold environment—like the inside of a fridge!

My next challenge is to introduce French to the curriculum. That's a possibility for me—at least at an introductory level. So I do a bit of that. However, the ultimate challenge comes when I am asked to teach some history—Nigerian history. All I know about Nigerian history is from a colonial perspective, and so with the aid of recently written indigenous history books, I begin to teach as requested, working one page ahead of my pupils. I find this interesting, and it leads me to reference several of Achebe's books charting the enormous social changes which occurred when Nigeria became independent from Britain, and how society was affected by a mass movement of villagers moving into the cities looking for paid employment.

The school has a fairly respectable library, the books having been donated by overseas charitable organisations. They are listed on the shelves alphabetically by author, but I have a better idea. I suggest they can be arranged according to the Dewey decimal classification system as there is, in fact, a book in the library outlining the process, and this is discussed at a staff meeting. Eventually, to everyone's relief, I "volunteer" to do it. I am also asked to give a brief description of the system to the boys at morning assembly. Maybe I need to learn to say "No" to my ever-expanding curricular responsibilities.

Surviving and Thriving

Chapter Five

Christmas and Bombs

When the school closes for the Christmas holidays, I look forward to yet another new experience: celebrating Christmas in the tropical heat, as opposed to the typical cold of a Scottish winter. We are invited to join expatriate neighbours for a Christmas meal and I am excited at the thought of tasting familiar food once more. I do like the cassava, yams, stews and "jollof rice" which Charity prepares for us, but it will be good to return to familiar-tasting dishes.

What I don't realise is that Christmas dinner in Nigeria, had we been visiting and eating with an Igbo family, is much the same as a Christmas dinner in Scotland. A traditional Nigerian Christmas dinner generally consists of roast chicken, rice instead of potatoes, roast vegetables, fresh fruit salad and palm wine with the meal. Not much difference there. So on Christmas day, we visit our neighbours and enjoy a traditional British meal where there is also the option of roast goat, seen as a local delicacy.

I sample the goat meat just to see what I am missing, following the saga of our stolen goat; it is different but quite delicious. Outside we hear the sound of firecrackers which is a local custom celebrating Christmas, and after our meal, we are entertained by a group of young girls who are going around the houses singing carols. They accompany their singing with "shekeres", which are percussion instruments consisting of dried gourds with beads woven into a loose net covering them. By holding the gourd in one hand and shaking it against the other, our carol singers produce a rhythmic sound from the beads striking the gourd with which to accompany their carols. The youngsters also dance to the rhythm they are producing, and they are all wearing their new Christmas dresses. Functional items such as soap, food items, and new clothes appear to be the norm in terms of gifts amongst the indigenous families.

During our meal, there are various conversations taking place. I overhear an interesting one around local culture, and Sennen is being asked for his input.

"Sennen, what is happening with your friend Chukwuemeka? I understand his wife Ingrid went on holiday back to Germany with their two boys and she is refusing to return?"

"It's really a very difficult situation, but in some ways quite straightforward. We value our children highly and so it is important for a couple to produce children, especially boys, as that is a type of insurance for a man's old age when the sons will look after him. We like to care for our own, so if a man decides to separate from his wife, she is not simply sent off to look after herself as they do in Europe. She will, instead, be sent back to her own family to be cared for by them in the future. It's that simple."

"But what about these children who are now in Germany? Who decides what should happen to them?"

"Obviously the children belong to the father, and he will be responsible for bringing them up. The mother has no rights in respect of taking the children with her when she goes. This is the Igbo way and always has been. As the head of my own family, I have a responsibility to look after my extended family also, to try and educate the younger ones and grow the family wealth. In other circumstances, the extended family would normally live with me. My own situation with Evelyn is a little bit different, so they are not here with us, but are back in the family home in the village with my mother who is widowed."

Sennen looks across at me and smiles. I have not heard this information before and was unaware of these additional financial responsibilities he is carrying. Perhaps this explains why his younger brother, who is at university, often visits, and there are conversations between them from which I am excluded.

One hot afternoon during the Christmas holidays, while relaxing on the balcony I am trying to decide whether to read another book or take a dip in our swimming pool.

I am half asleep but subconsciously hearing a distant rumbling. It's similar to the sound of the freight lorries that struggle to climb the hill beyond our estate. I am waiting for the gear change which will indicate the lorry has reached the summit. However, the "rumbling" continues for an extended period of time, and on opening my eyes I realise there is no lorry. Instead, I observe a plane slowly approaching up the valley. Curiosity compels me to watch the progress of the plane as we don't live on a flight path. As it draws nearer I see the door of the plane opening and something like tennis balls falling out. It takes me just one nano-second to realise that what I am seeing are not tennis balls. They are bombs! And the plane is heading directly for the nearby electricity power station—a bombing raid is in progress. Panic-stricken I run, yelling for Charity, and we hide in the space below the staircase, hoping and praying that the house will not be hit. Thoughts and fears are galloping through my head and my heart is pounding.

Is Sennen safe at the power station? What about the village close to the station? Is the leprosy settlement in danger? How many casualties will there be? How will people get to a hospital?

Then I pause and think:

I didn't hear any explosions, or did I miss hearing them in my panic? What on earth is going on, and how can I find out—if we ever dare come out of hiding?

We later discover that several bombs have fallen in the forest and did not explode. There has been no damage to property and no injuries to individuals. But the incident provides much food for thought. When Sennen eventually returns home that evening, he is extremely disturbed and concerned for everyone's safety, both here at home, and also at the power station. He assumes that this was an attempt to destroy the power station, and it is very likely to be repeated. The question is how soon might that be? That evening we listen to the BBC World News and are astounded and shocked to hear: "The Nigerian Air Force today launched a successful bombing raid targeting the Oji River Power Station. Ten square miles around the station has been razed and the operation is being hailed as a major success."

This report was transmitted on the BBC World News from Lagos, five hundred miles west of Oji River. As locals, we know it is untrue and merely a propaganda exercise.

My thoughts go immediately to my parents back in Scotland, who may also be hearing this broadcast, and I wonder how they might be reacting to such news, not knowing the reality of the situation. There is no option if we are to be safe. We have to move.

Our inquiries start, and we are not reassured when all of the expatriates on site are summoned home by their various embassies. I'm confused by this. It seems like a knee jerk reaction. The British embassy also alerts the UK citizens in the eastern region, advising all of us to leave, and so many of my friends and contacts prepare to go.

For me to leave is unthinkable. I am married and I fully trust my husband to do what is needed to keep me safe. Retrospectively I now realise that my trust was misplaced as there was little he could do in the ensuing chaos which engulfed the region. I also did not like being told what to do by officials without any recognition of our individual circumstances or any consultation.

In this, my exciting, challenging, busy, self-centred existence, I have not been listening to any news or political comment or reading any national newspapers, and I fail to realise that the 1960s independence has not brought unity and peace to Nigeria. When the British established the original boundaries that would delineate the country, they ignored the many tribal differences that existed across the area, particularly when amalgamating the northern with the southern areas. As with other similar colonial situations throughout the world, group loyalties are threatened by forced amalgamation, and this often leads to intense rivalries in respect of tribal self-determination and power. The north, the east and the west in Nigeria are all divided into tribal loyalties by the River Niger and its two tributaries, creating a "Y-type" formation. There are also religious allegiances along the same lines. The largest area, the north, is populated by members of the Hausa tribe who are mainly Moslem. The eastern Igbo people are predominantly Christian, and the west is a mix of both religions among the Yoruba tribe. There are also smaller groups in all the areas practising older traditional animistic religions. The Igbos were quick to adopt a western-style education which was introduced by the early missionaries, and as a result, following independence, well-educated Igbos are to be found in many of the top military and civil administration posts, particularly in Lagos, but also in the other regional capital towns throughout the country.

Events are beginning to take on a pattern, based on tribal loyalties, with the Igbos being seen as the "bad guys." Some groups are objecting to the dominance of Igbos in senior positions, and relationships are deteriorating. I am almost completely oblivious to these rumblings and the animosity which is growing—especially between the Christian east and the Muslim north. Rumours abound in the east, one of which details the possibility of tins of evaporated milk being poisoned prior to them entering the area. We all begin to examine our milk tins, to ascertain whether the tin is smooth or there is a suspicious looking "blob" on the base which would be indicative of interference. Thoughts also arise about potential food blockages, as much of the food comes into the east across the bridge on the Niger and it would, therefore, be a simple matter to blockade lorries carrying food supplies. We feel it may be wise to take some protective action ourselves and make sure we don't run out of certain food supplies. So we buy a full bag of rice, and stock up on tinned meat, dried fish, uncontaminated tins of milk and any other items which can be stored long term. Others are taking the same measures to protect themselves and their families. No-one is being honest when asked about how much they have stored, the fear is that they may have to share at some later date, and thus diminish what they have for themselves. This leads me to think: *We are all in the same boat, so when it's gone it's gone, and sharing will be better than seeing someone starve to death when we could help.*

I believe now that Sennen was trying his best to protect me in some way from the speed at which events were moving. He did not tell me about the military coup in Lagos when Igbo generals deposed the Nigerian federal government over allegations of massive corruption. Six months later a counter-coup was then undertaken by Northerners who felt the Igbos were gaining too much national power. Soon after this second coup events cannot be ignored, as the radio begins broadcasting the disturbing news of Igbos being massacred in the north on the streets of the towns where they were living and working. Igbos, who are Christian and well educated, are scattered across all the regions in the country, running successful businesses and working in government jobs. This creates jealousy, hostility and antagonism. We hear that bands of Northerners are rampaging in the streets and summarily executing Igbos. They are also searching the homes of Igbos and executing them there. There is justifiably a massive concern in the east around these killings, and soon the remaining Igbos from other areas begin running for their lives, returning to the east. Trains, planes and lorries transport thousands of Igbo individuals and families back to their homeland. Panic is taking over everywhere. Even within the eastern state, schools are closing as pupils abandon their studies and return in fear to their families. This includes the students at Achi, so my job is lost. Many of those returning from the north who have family or relatives around Oji River arrive at the power station seeking help, and we are able to run a soup kitchen from the house to try and ease the immediate desperation of the returning people. This is when I am so glad we have stockpiled food and can make this provision. Stories of the horrors and atrocities the returnees have witnessed and experienced, lead to mounting anger among the Igbos, and talk begins of the need for the protection of their homeland—the eastern state—and the strengthening of the military in the area. It has been estimated that a million Igbos lost their lives during this period. Meanwhile, supplies of planes and armaments are being provided by the British government in an attempt to shore up the Nigerian federal government which is based in Lagos.

Chapter Six

Evacuate from Oji to Enugu to Akeme - Uno

As expatriate managers leave the power station and return to their respective countries it becomes apparent that the station will need to be shut down, so Sennen is able to de-commission the operating plant and secure the site against looting or other malicious damage. He then turns his attention to our personal situation and within a few months has negotiated access to a friend's unoccupied flat in Enugu. A Swiss engineer living beside us, who is evacuating on the advice of his embassy, leaves us the amazing gift of his treasured two-seater sports car. He tells us, "When you feel your life may be at stake, possessions seem somehow much less relevant, so please have my car."

This proves to be an important pronouncement that I will find myself returning to at a later date.

Having concluded the Enugu deal we can now plan our departure from Oji River. I have been here for just over three years and it's hard to be going into another unknown, but I still have that adventurous spirit, and I do still feel safe with Sennen. I don't know what's in his mind about employment, but I decide not to ask.

"Now that we have two cars we can take more personal belongings as we move to Enugu, so we have to think carefully about what to pack and take," announces Sennen.

"Is the flat furnished?" I want to know.

"As far as I know, it is fully furnished, but we will need to take other things that might be needed. If you and Charity try and sort out the domestic side of things I will deal with the other stuff."

"What do you mean by 'other stuff'?"

"Well, we have important documents such as our passports, UK driving licenses, bank books, university degree papers and a few other bits and pieces. The plan is that I will organise these papers and store them in a briefcase, which will always be the first item to be lifted and saved in any ensuing emergency."

"What about my geological specimens? I really don't want to lose them. You do know the fossils constitute a significant and valuable collection?"

"Get serious Evelyn. You don't really think they are all that important under the circumstances, do you?"

I realise it's a rhetorical question and so I keep my thoughts to myself, in spite of my annoyance. *I sometimes wonder what kind of confusion there will be in decades to come when fossils from around Britain are "discovered" in West Africa. Was Darwin's theory right or wrong after all?*

So with the two cars at our disposal, we are able to pack bed linen, towels, clothes, pots and pans and all the basics we require to set up home again. Just one week later, Sennen, Charity and I head off to a new home with our two cars.

We are not in Enugu for more than a month when Charity comes to us in tears saying she wants to go back to her family in the village. We wonder whether she will actually be more at risk there, rather than staying with us. We are beginning to hear sporadic gunshots in the distance and I think this is possibly spooking her. She does not like town life, never before having lived in a large settlement. So, in the end, we agree to her request and Sennen sets off with Charity, taking her back to her kinsfolk in a distant village. On his return journey, he runs into aggressive armed individuals at a roadblock. This is Igbo territory, he is an Igbo and so he is able to by-pass this barrier, but the experience un-nerves him. These armed villagers who have stopped him are expecting to have to repel approaching Nigerians. They can all hear gunshots in the distance and anxiety levels are high, hence Sennen being stopped and questioned. To avoid further dangers he re-routes to come back via barely passable jungle tracks, and in so doing manages to avoid more roadblocks on the main routes.

While I am alone with my thoughts I clench my fists

in frustration and screw up my face. My so-called earlier "adventure" has long since disappeared and is being thwarted by politics and fighting. I am angry. My situation is no longer as engaging as it was when we first arrived in the country. Now the distant sounds of hostilities are even causing families in Enugu to consider moving back to *their* villages and away from the town, which is suspected of being a possible target of the Nigerian army. There have been reports of skirmishes around Onitsha, with the Nigerian army having succeeded in crossing the River Niger into the Eastern Region, and then having been repelled back across the river into the Mid-Western State. It is hard to ascertain the truth of these rumours, but people are becoming more and more distressed by what they hear. While waiting for Sennen to return, I am visited by several of our friends who are in an obvious state of alarm, "Evelyn, where is Sennen?"

"He's not here. He has gone with Charity back to her village because she was so fearful and wanted to return to her family."

"Will you come with us then? We are apprehensive about where the fighting is, and we think the town may be about to fall into the hands of the Nigerians. No Igbo will be safe when that happens."

"I can't go with you without Sennen. How will he know where I am if he returns and I'm not here? I need to wait for him to come back for me."

"Please come with us. We can't wait any longer because of the risks."

"No, I'm sorry but I am going to wait for Sennen."

And so I spend several anxious, angry and frightened hours waiting alone, hearing more gunfire and wondering if I have made the right decision.

As night begins to fall I become really concerned about the duration of Sennen's absence. Should I have gone to safety with his friends? I pace around the flat, unable to focus on anything other than my sore head and palpitating heart. It is midnight when he finally returns. His experiences have so shocked him he makes the decision that we need to move again and immediately. My pulse begins to race. *Oh no. Not again. Two moves in less than three months!* So many dramatic changes are happening after such a brief idyllic sojourn of just three years in Oji River. To my utter dismay, this time it will be back to the native village Akeme Uno where Sennen's widowed mother still lives. This location being more central within the eastern region is thus further away and safer from current border skirmishes. The Nigerian Federal Government, meanwhile, is tightening its grip on the eastern region and is starting to blockade the boundaries. Cameroon, the country to the east has closed its border with Nigeria, and these various moves have resulted in a drastic reduction of food supplies. For many people, starvation is fast becoming a reality. Rural villages are faring a little better as subsistence farming is a way of life for the villagers, but pressure from returning family members is also affecting their levels of available food supplies. It is becoming apparent that an attempt to starve the population is one of the war strategies being used to bring about submission and defeat.

So we pack the cars yet again and hasten to leave Enugu. I am just becoming accustomed to listening for the distant sound of warfare and wanting to be as far away from it as I possibly can be. We set off. I am driving our sports car and following Sennen. Less than half a mile after leaving our parking lot outside the flat, my car has a puncture! This is disastrous, but there is no question about how to react. The briefcase containing our papers is in Sennen's car, so it is a simple matter to jump out of my car and join him in the other one. I clearly recall the message from our Swiss benefactor regarding safety versus possessions, and now I find myself in just that very situation. Bed linen, towels, clothes, all the softer items in the sports car are simply abandoned. It's hard to describe the emotions that run through me at this point. *What have I let myself in for by marrying and coming to live in Africa? Were my parents right after all? What's happened to the luxurious lifestyle to which I was becoming accustomed only a few months before? Is it only months? It feels like years. Where will Sennen find alternative employment, if indeed he can? Where will the money come from? When might it all end? How can I handle this? Is it all a bad dream? Would that it were!!*

Living with one's mother-in-law can be tricky for some wives and people like to joke about it, but when it comes to the bit and I realise just how basic this new situation in the village is, I know for sure that I'm one who may find it rather difficult. That's putting it mildly. Believe me, it is no joke. First problem—language. Although I speak some Igbo, the language, being tonal, reduces most of my efforts to communicate with Mother to gibberish. Second problem—cooking. I am allocated an outdoor kitchen with an open wood fire to cook for Sennen, while Mother cooks for herself. The young children from our extended family in the village are responsible for fetching the wood for our separate fires, and I'm grateful that I was an accomplished Girl Guide when it came to camping and cooking outdoors on an open fire. These past experiences are serving me well in this new context.

"Why is she taking such large peelings from the yam? She wastes so much food." is one of mother's many complaints. Am I ever going to win? I think not!

Sennen and I have been married just over three years at this point, and I now face further derision and accusation about my lack of pregnancy.

"How can a so-called intelligent, educated white person not even know for sure whether or not she is pregnant?" complains Mother.

Suggesting that I thought I might be pregnant, in the hope that it would please Mother, simply back-fires on me.

The only positive in our situation is that we seem to be safe here in Akeme-Uno, but we are far from happy.

There is no running water in our compound, so again young relatives have tasks to fulfil. They are obliged to visit the nearest streams and bring back buckets of fresh water. To have a "bath"—outside in the yard of course—I take my bucket of water into the square construction of palm fronds which serves as a private area and begin to wash. I am wearing a blouse and a native wrapper, the traditional style of dress. It's an easy, cool and comfortable way to dress. By tossing my wrapper across the top of the palm fronds, I indicate that I am using the bathing enclosure. The young children who are usually around, come and peak through the fronds when I am washing—I suspect to see if I'm white all over! Should I mention the toileting arrangements? Well, Girl Guide experience to the rescue once more. Having camped in the countryside at home, a trench latrine is not unknown to me. But I won't describe the differences between there and here! Hygiene is a priority, even in the poorest of families, so a coconut half shell covers a pit latrine to keep the flies out. In this way, the pit is kept as hygienic as possible. The half shell is removed when in use and quickly replaced when one is finished. Enough said.

When in the compound cooking, I keep seeing three kitchen areas under the palm fronds and wonder why three, so I decide to enquire.

"Sennen, why are there several cooking areas outside when there is normally only your mother here at home?"

"Mmm, it's a long story. Some other time perhaps."

"We have all the time in the world if we choose to talk, so please, fill me in with this so-called long story."

"Oh well. The compound here and the adjoining farmland have been in our family for a long time. It goes so far back that the original house was built of mud. You've seen other mud houses elsewhere in the village, so you know what I'm talking about."

"Yes, I have seen them, but why the three kitchens for one house? Your mother uses one, I use another, and the third one seems never to be used, and looks like it is a long time since it was last used."

"When my father inherited the land, it was still a mud house, but having been educated by missionaries, he had secured work with a regular income, and he was able to demolish the old house and build the current one with breeze blocks and the tin roof. That's why there is enough room for us as well as for Mother. My father eventually rose to a position of company director and that's why he saw the potential for me if I was well educated."

"You are avoiding the question of the three kitchens. Why won't you just tell me?"

"It's difficult for you to understand because you don't really know our culture."

"I will try to understand if you will just please tell me."

"My father was a polygamist, as was the culture in his day. He was a wealthy man and so he married three wives. When he came under the influence of the missionaries and converted to Christianity, he had to decide what to do about his wives, so he selected my mother and sent the other two back to their families to be cared for by them. That's why there are three kitchens. Wives were not expected to share the cooking for their husband, and it avoided any quarrelling amongst them. It's also why there are three rooms in the house."

"Do you think you might improve the living conditions for your mother and build a better house?

"No. I don't think so. Mother is elderly and is used to how things are. It would be cruel to expect her to change, and it would upset the dynamic in the village, as I will not be living here permanently."

"Well, I found that quite interesting, and now I know more about both the culture and your family history. I don't understand why it was so difficult to tell me."

Chapter Seven

Biafra Declares Independence
(May 30th 1967 The Ahiara Declaration)

Sennen is well aware of just how awkward I am finding things living here in the village, so deploying his initiative yet again he begins to plan our next move. We do not have a joint discussion about this. Once more I am angry at being side-lined over issues which deeply concern and involve me. *Why won't he talk to me?* By this stage, political events are having a profound effect on the eastern region. Fighting and bombing, supported by the British government, represent attempts to force an acceptance of unity across all regions, and the town of Onitsha on the eastern side of the Niger has finally fallen to the federal government troops. Gradually they are encroaching further and further into the eastern territory. The southern coast line around Port Harcourt also falls to the Nigerians. We are now landlocked, but there is still a determination among the Igbos to protect themselves and their homeland. Momentously, on May 30th 1967 Colonel Emeka Ojukwu, the military governor of the region, declares cessation from Nigeria and names the territory Biafra. He later documented his insights and plans in a small booklet: The Ahiara Declaration sub-titled 'the principles of the Biafran Revolution', by Emeka Ojukwu, General of the People's Army.

In July of the same year, the Federal Government of Nigeria responded with an official declaration of war. The borders of Biafra are now totally blockaded and this means *no* food supplies or armaments can enter the east. We are going to have to try and exist in a fully land-locked and diminishing territory. This smacks of planned genocide—and the Biafran armed forces have no recourse to external military support.

It takes another four months for Sennen to explore the possibilities of some kind of personal employment and safety for us both. Before leaving Akeme Uno I now know that I am definitely pregnant, but with no access to medical support I'm not too sure of the stage I am at. We are both thrilled at the prospect of finally starting our family and ask God for the protection we will need to see this pregnancy through to a successful birth. There has been so much pressure on us both to produce a child, but the timing does not feel entirely propitious, what with the fighting, the shortages of food and the other privations we are enduring.

Sennen finally resolves his employment situation by offering his engineering skills to the Biafran resistance army, but he does not sign up for their military service, preferring instead to work as a civilian. The post he is offered takes us to the south-east town of Abakiliki—an area where expatriates have previously been in charge of zinc mining. On their evacuation at the start of the troubles, the mines, due to lack of maintenance became flooded—not with pure water but with brine. Sennen's role is to find a way of extracting salt from the mines and rendering it usable for human consumption. With the blockades in place, there has been no salt available for quite some time and so it is becoming a high priority. Not only will the salt be used in cooking but also as a preservative when drying meat and fish. This "posting" comes with accommodation attached—a furnished bungalow with fully functioning air-conditioning, typical of the standard housing allocated to professional expatriates. I smile at the irony of having electricity from a small local generator and a cooker but no food to cook on it.

I soon discover that there is a small abandoned library on site, so I make frequent visits there and simply take what I want to read, returning and replacing books as I choose, since there is no supervision in place. It is becoming a frequent experience to realise I am the only white person, "onyeocha", in each of the areas where we end up living. I ask myself: *Why am I still here?* "I'm married" is the obvious answer. "I'm expecting our child" is another. The ultimate reason is that I don't know how to do anything independently about my situation, even though I no longer see this type of life as an adventure. I hardly see it as life at all; it is so difficult and dangerous with no apparent answers. We have long since lost any semblance of community fellowship, and holding on to our faith is a challenge. We pray, and we pray, and we pray for peace, but it seems our prayers are going unheard. God's timing is not man's timing and it's hard to wait patiently for answers.

By now I suspect that I'm around four or five months pregnant. I'm unsure as I have no medical supervision in place. Food has become a major issue for us, as most of the time we have no food at all, and we only eat when someone local brings food to us. This is becoming a very desperate time. Igbo culture dictates that a pregnant woman should have the best of food and plenty of it, so local people try to be kind to me as they can see I am pregnant and when they do have any food to share they bring some to me. One day workmen arrive and offer me some dried snake meat. They tell me they have been home near to Port Harcourt and brought back some dried food to share. While I thank them for the "snake meat", they are laughing and joking with each other in their own language, and from the little I understand, they appear to be laughing at the fact they've deceived me by pretending that dried human meat is snake meat. When Sennen returns I ask,

"What is this joke about Port Harcourt and dried snake or human meat, and which is it?"

"Port Harcourt is currently under Nigerian control, so it's unlikely the men were actually in the town, but it is an area where cannibalism was generally practised in the recent past. Meat is meat, so let's not worry about its origin. It's unlikely that it is actually human meat."

This time he's not mad at me, but glad to accept any kind of food from whoever brought it to us, and from wherever it came. So that evening we cook and enjoy a rare meal of rice and meat.

Yet again I'm bored, or is it depression? There is so little I can or need to do, so I spend a lot of time lying in bed, just resting and reading. The one sound I am constantly alert to is the distant sound of fighting, but for now, it does seem to be very far away, so there is no immediate need for concern or panic. One day, relaxing in the bedroom and quietly reading, I hear a scraping sound against the outside of the bedroom wall. Immediately on high alert, I slip quietly to the floor hiding on the far side of the bed. There are men outside the house. *What are they after?* As I watch from my hiding place, I see the air-conditioning unit disappear out through the wall and a final heave disconnects the plug from the socket. Looters! At least they are only after "things" and not after me. I breathe an extra sigh of relief recognising that they do not appear to be Nigerians.

We remain here for longer than we have been anywhere else since leaving Oji River. I spend a lot of time catching up on classics I haven't read before: "The Catcher in the Rye", "Of Mice and Men", and I re-read some old favourites: "Black Beauty" and "Don Quixote". The familiarity of these books creates a sense of nostalgia, occupies my thoughts and helps to keep me calm. Lying in bed reading, I still hear sounds of fighting in the distance, and week by week they are definitely closing in on us. The time is undoubtedly coming when we will need to be on the move yet again! By now I am probably around seven months pregnant and not putting on any weight due to lack of food. When I allow myself a bit of introspection I realise I *am* becoming really depressed about this whole sorry saga.

So where to, and when will the next move happen? As the salt production is a military-backed opportunity for Sennen he looks to the army for support. We are therefore able to move when the time comes and the fighting is closing in on us. This time it is to an army camp in yet another area of the country away from the front line. Typically the army personnel are occupying a group of deserted bungalows, and we are offered a caravan on the same site next to one of the bungalows. No fancy home this time. We are fortunate still to have our car and access to petrol from the military. As we travel to take up residence in our 'new home' this time we recognise that the number of people fleeing on foot has increased dramatically. They too are looking for safety, but for them, it will be the next refugee camp. Ironically it helps sustain me to realise that we have yet to reach the level of deprivation that these poor native people are experiencing.

Again, with little to do, I lie in bed and sleep a lot. The caravan is like an oven in the daytime and an icebox at night. The only time we eat is when the soldiers next door have food and are willing to share with us. Not even the military people have adequate or regular food supplies, and so the sharing with us is pretty sporadic. I grow increasingly concerned about my weight, but there is nothing we can do about it. Our only option is to survive as best we can. I reflect on our Christian commitment and deeply regret the loss of church and fellowship. I ask myself, "Where is God in all this suffering?" We have witnessed the constant movement and increasing numbers of people searching for the next refugee camp. They carry large bundles on their heads in the traditional way, children are crying as they accompany their parents, and everyone is showing signs of weakness, illness, and starvation.

Sennen is once more on engineering duty with the army, but, as has become his pattern, he does not share any information about his new tasks with me. He uses military vehicles when he goes out daily and leaves me in the caravan. Our own car has a full tank of petrol but is up on jacks for security. The critical time it will next be used is when I need to get to a hospital to deliver our child. A local woman has spotted me in the army camp and has organised the fetching of water for me—two buckets a day, brought by children who have been to the local stream to fetch it. At least it is possible to have a wash, but we are back once more to pit latrines, this time with less privacy.

Wearied again by this seemingly pointless depressing existence— no nearby library this time—I feel desperate to have something, anything to do, so I discuss it with Sennen. I am hoping he will work out a solution, and true to form he finds an answer. He negotiates a role for me in association with NGO relief workers who visit the many refugee camps which are growing across the remaining Biafran territory. Relief supplies are being flown in sporadically from overseas countries including Scotland. The planes are at risk from the anti-aircraft fire on the southern coastal border at Port Harcourt, but there are brave pilots willing to face this risk on humanitarian grounds. Among the supplies, there are huge reels of thick cotton thread, bolts of cloth and of course medical supplies—especially vitamins—to try and help with the health issues associated with starvation, particularly for the children. Aid workers have their base near to where we are living and they offer me "work". They provide a driver to pick me up and return me to the caravan when finished for the day. It feels good to talk to British and European people again, the aid workers from the NGOs in the area. My role initially is to count vitamin tablets into sevens and fourteens, package them into small plastic bags and box them, ready for distribution to the refugee camps. I'm delighted to have something to occupy me, even such a routine task as this. Several other local Biafran volunteers also work with me, and I'm given the role of overseeing the process. My being given this position of "authority" is an indication to the others that I will be watching for any stealing or dishonesty and it will not be tolerated. Racketeering is rife as everyone is suffering so much. The vitamins could be sold on the black market, or used personally; people are really desperate. Other tasks I am given include the production of small garments for infants in the camps. I do this "at home" with a hand operated Singer sewing machine which is gifted to me by a Dutch doctor who is returning to Holland at the end of her tour of duty. Her one stipulation when giving me the machine is that I will not simply abandon it, but make sure it continues to be used for some positive purpose. Being a fairly competent seamstress, it is a pleasure for me to be able to sew tiny shift dresses and small trousers for those destitute and heart-breaking refugee children. I am also given some of the reels of the heavy cotton thread, and by trebling strands of it, I am able to produce bootees and knitted cardigans, both for our own child and for the camps. One surprise which surfaces among the relief supplies has come from Germany. Hundreds of brown paper packages looking creased and old are stamped with swastikas giving an indication of their age. Each package contains several metres of wide gauze from which I am able to produce nappies by stitching several layers together, again for ourselves and others. I continue with these tasks until I give birth some weeks later. My local friendly lady is keeping an eye on me as my pregnancy develops, and she gives me lots of advice and signs to watch for that will indicate my "time" is approaching.

Chapter Eight

A War-time Birth

When my waters do break I am home alone and begin to panic. *Help! How do I deal with this on my own?* Then I calm down a little and start to consider my options. I'm aware the nearest maternity hospital is about eighty miles away. We have previously discussed this and decided that is where I should go to give birth. But where is Sennen when I need him? I wonder about seeking help from the nearby soldiers who have transport available. *Should I go to them and ask for help?* It seems like a no-brainer, so I approach them. I'm in the middle of explaining my dilemma and trying to negotiate with them when Sennen returns. I am so grateful for his appearance! I now feel much better and more secure as I know we have our own transport and a full tank. Sennen checks the car, prepares it for the journey and we set off.

We make a good start, but about ten miles into our travels a tropical storm overtakes us. Rain batters the windscreen turning it into frosted glass, and the wipers can barely cope, even on the high speed setting. This is slowing us down and now my contractions are coming so close together that I begin to doubt if we will reach the hospital in time. I should alert Sennen to my situation. However, rather than distract him from his driving I choose to remain silent and pray, hoping against hope that I can hold out for the duration of the journey.

When we finally arrive at the hospital, my admission is processed promptly. We have made it in time and a few hours later I give birth to a beautiful daughter weighing a healthy 6lbs 12 oz. We name her Ngozi, which means "Blessing". My own weight drops dramatically following the birth, and I find myself unable to feed her. *What is going to happen now?* Relief supplies are the answer. The hospital staff bring me a daily supply of dried milk powder, and I learn how to be a new mother. I thank God for this provision donated by caring people from around the world. I also enjoy a morning cup of tea and freshly baked scones on a daily basis. What a luxury *that* is. The hospital is run by the Catholic Church and many of the staff are nuns from overseas. Aid workers generally have reasonable food supplies to meet their basic needs in order to equip them for duty; as a result, while in hospital, patients' diets are also reasonable. I spend long hours just looking into the crib and admiring the baby lying peacefully there. She will never know the drama and traumas of the previous nine months or the ongoing fear for all our safety. A couple of days later I awake with a raging temperature, and I am diagnosed with malaria. I have forgotten to bring my prophylactics with me, and as I examine the mosquito net around my bed, I can see the holes where the mosquitoes have secured their access to me. This delays my discharge. As if this is not bad enough, I am terror-stricken when a few days later I hear what I think is the distant droning of an aircraft. I sense the sound approaching, and as it grows louder, confirming my fears, I begin to panic and then recall that I need to follow the instructions that we have all been given in the event of an air raid.

"Take the pillow from your bed and place it on the floor. Lift the baby from the crib and place her on the pillow. Slide the pillow under the bed and slip below the bed yourself, protecting the baby with your own body."

I do as required but I am trembling in fear and agony. Am I to lose this baby after only four days, having taken four years to conceive? I cry aloud to God for mercy, my hot tears flowing down onto the baby. I am drained of hope and utterly helpless in this situation. *How can I survive this critical ordeal? Is this to be the end? Will the baby survive?* But survive we do. Others in the hospital are less fortunate. In the panic of the raid, surgeons flee for cover, abandoning their operating theatres and their patients. Others run outside screaming in terror, and hoping they will be safe if the buildings are hit. It is well recognised that the Nigerians are targeting hospitals on the mistaken assumption that

Biafran soldiers are hiding there. Fortunately—or unfortunately, depending on how you view it—the damage to the buildings is minimal, but the strafing from the departing plane kills many of those who chose the outside as the safer option. I cannot wait for Sennen to come and take us back to the relative safety of the caravan. *But what will happen about milk for Ngozi?*

As we prepare to leave the hospital I am given a seven day supply of powdered milk. We thank the staff for our care and for the milk, making haste to be on our way. We have to trust that boiling the water which the youngster delivers to us from the nearby stream means it can be used safely to prepare milk for the baby. However, relief at all being back together is short lived. Six days later we look at one another and the unspoken question between us is, *What about tomorrow when the supply of powdered milk runs out?* We really have no answer to this. *What are we going to do?* Time for some serious prayer. Is God seeing the desolation around us? Does he recognise our personal misery at this moment? Will he intervene and bring some kind of sanity into the situation? It's hard to continue to have faith when things have been so terrible for so long. But God is good, and miracles do happen! The following day one of the nuns from the hospital arrives by car - a 160-mile round trip. She brings us a seven-day supply of powdered milk. It feels like a miracle. It *is* a miracle - an answer to our desperate prayers. And so we stagger like this from one week to the next, constantly wondering how long we can keep our daughter alive. During one of the deliveries of milk powder, I am moved to suggest,

"Sister, if we receive half the quantity of milk powder, then another infant could also benefit from the other half." The nun's response severely chastens me.

"What you don't realise is the constant dilemma we face in deciding who gets the milk - basically who lives and who dies. When a child is born healthy, we do our best to support the continuing health of that child. That is why *you* are supplied with all the milk that you need. That will continue as long as we are getting relief supplies from overseas. We see many children with such a poor birth weight that they have no hope of survival when returning to the camps, and the decision to withhold supplies in those circumstances is heart-breaking. There are also older children being brought to the hospital for treatment by their mothers. Some of these children are turned away in the knowledge that they also have no chance of recovery. Can you understand how devastating these decisions are for us as well as for the parents? When you sign up to the Hippocratic Oath you do not expect to have to make such decisions so frequently. So, no more daft ideas about sharing your supplies. I hope to visit you again next week. 'Till then, goodbye."

So we stumble from week to week like this, wondering how to keep our daughter alive should relief supplies fail.

By the time she is three months old and already being supplemented with watery mashed banana we make a momentous decision. Our agonising dilemma is whether we can sustain our marriage and stay together in the continuing Biafran rebellion and lose Ngozi, or whether I should return to Scotland and thus save her life. A heart-breaking choice! Separation from my husband feels like a cruel conclusion to our marriage, albeit temporarily. Escape from the war with Ngozi is a frightening but welcome idea. There is no doubt that motherhood changes one forever, and the maternal protective instinct is very much at the forefront of my thoughts. The reality is that for our child to survive I need to return with her back to Scotland and so the decision is made.

Chapter Nine

I Return to Scotland with Ngozi

I wonder what my parents know or hear about the war.
I can only wonder, but they are after all 'family' and I
do miss them—even my three brothers.

We assume that it may take some time to procure the necessary documents for me to travel, thus giving ourselves a short window of time to try and adjust mentally and emotionally to the forthcoming separation. A few days later we venture back to Owerri to investigate travel plans for myself and Ngozi. I have a British passport, and with the baby being female, we should both be able to leave with minimal difficulties. Sennen, as a Biafran male, will not be granted permission to leave, and we are aware of this. In the first office we go to, my passport is checked; the necessary accompanying documents are processed and given to me. We are then instructed to report to another office where travel plans will be arranged for us. As we make our way there, we are caught up in a bombing raid on the town and there is panic everywhere—people running up side streets, trying to judge where the jets are overhead, and where the bombs might fall. We, too, take cover. Time passes and it seems the raid is over, but panic and uncertainty remain. People begin tentatively to emerge and resume their activities. We know bombs have been dropped, but we have not heard explosions. This is a particularly wicked raid, as when people do begin to appear out of hiding the explosions start to boom around us. Delayed timers in the bombs have confounded and confused us about our safety. Eventually, when we decide it is safe to move on, we finally locate the office to which we have been directed. It turns out that this is Biafra's air transport control base. The haste with which we are processed reinforces the ongoing fear and uncertainty. The office staff are obviously in a hurry to vacate the building and to be somewhere that they feel may be safer. They tell us that a Swedish plane bringing aid from the churches there is expected that evening. It will land on the main highway outside the town as the airstrip has been bombed, and it may be my last chance of getting out. My papers receive a very cursory examination. I am handed a letter and instructed:

"Read that and be on the plane tonight! There may not be another!"

"Be on it!" is the insistent message. The letter I am given is addressed to the churches in Sweden, requesting that I be repatriated to Scotland.

It suddenly strikes me that we have not been using any money since we left Enugu and in fact, although the Biafran government has produced its own currency it will not be recognised beyond the borders. Any food we have recently eaten has been given to us and Sennen has been using military vehicles supplied with petrol. I am about to become a penniless refugee heading for my own country.

We return to the caravan and consider what I will take with me. I pack a small bag with a minimum of necessities, I lift the sewing machine and ....

"What are you doing?" is the immediate reaction. "You can't possibly lug that thing around with you on a plane!"

"Yes I can, and I will. I made a promise to the Dutch doctor when she was leaving and gave me the machine. This is my way of honouring that promise. I'm leaving with no money, but this machine can prove to be an earner for me back in Scotland."

"What is that supposed to mean? What use is an old out-dated sewing machine going to be for you?"

"Who made the curtains for our home in Oji River? Who made the casual shirts for you in the fabric of your choice? Who sewed all these garments for the refugee children in the camps? Have you not seen enough of my work to realise I am an accomplished seamstress and could make a living using my skills?"

"Oh, hurry up then. Stop wasting time. We need to be on our way."

I'm sure this lack of reasoned discussion between us is all stress related to the suddenness surrounding my departure. We have not had the "luxury" of the two weeks or so that we thought we had when we might have tried to come to terms with our forced separation. We prepare to leave and we travel in silence, immersed in our own thoughts until we eventually reach the road serving as the departure point where we find the plane waiting. There is an urgent request for me to get on board. With only a curt and hasty "Goodbye," between us I climb aboard the plane with Ngozi, the sewing machine and my empty wallet. I feel totally and utterly abandoned and destitute.

I am now alone in the world with a three-month-old child and no financial support. I look around for a seat on the plane and realise there are no seats. They have all been removed to maximise storage space for incoming aid supplies, so I sit on the floor with Ngozi on my lap and lean against the side of the plane. It feels bitterly cold and very scary. I realise I am trembling, both from the cold of the metal at my back and with apprehension about the unknown into which I am travelling. There are several others on board but I don't speak to anyone. They may, like me, be escaping from the war zone. They could be aid workers going on furlough. I'm too emotionally exhausted to care. *I wonder how long the flight to Sweden will be, and whether it's a direct flight. Will anything ever sort itself out in the future for us? Will I ever see Sennen again? Will Ngozi see her father again, and if so, when? Is the nightmare of the last two years over, or is there more to come?*

As the plane takes off it heads south. Suddenly, in the darkness beyond the plane, I see bursts of colour in the sky. Surely it can't be fireworks?

Someone yells, "We're crossing the border! The Nigerians are targeting us with anti-aircraft guns along the coastline."

We fly through this fierce and prolonged fire before finally landing safely on the island of San Tome in the Gulf of Biafra. There we leave the plane and are all escorted to a safe house—"we" being departing aid workers, journalists, myself and Ngozi. I don't know why, but the plane will not leave again for three days. There are others already in the safe house and it is here that I meet another Scot: Dr Clyne Shepherd. He is heading back to Edinburgh via Frankfurt. While in Frankfurt he is booked to talk to church leaders in an ongoing effort to increase help for the desperate conditions prevailing in the refugee camps in Biafra. He has been working in the Queen Elizabeth Hospital in Umuahia and is hugely affected by what he experienced there. It echoes the heartbreak of the Owerri Hospital staff. He speaks movingly of turning away many children because they are going to die in spite of any care that the hospital can offer. How devastating is that for a man committed to saving lives? Dr Shepherd is kind enough to pay for our food and to help with Ngozi during

75

the three days we spend at the safe house. He also vacates his bedroom for me and instead he sleeps on a mattress among the other men in the lounge. I am so appreciative of this, as I am the only female here.

Eventually, we are back on the same plane, still without seats, and heading for Sweden via Frankfurt, where we will land and refuel. When we arrive in Germany the plane is besieged by journalists eager for news about the war situation. Having managed to avoid this scrum and reach a rest area, I am simply planning to refresh myself and Ngozi. In the rest room, another traveller speaks to me and kindly offers to hold her while I see to my own needs. The moment she is out of my arms I flop and go down and out like a light! Is it the strangeness of being back among Europeans, or simply of being out of Africa? My collapse creates some consternation and when I recover I am asked:

"Why are you on this particular relief plane and what were you doing in Biafra?"

The answer is simple. "I am escaping the war with my child and I have a letter to the Swedish churches asking them to repatriate me back to Scotland, so I have no alternative."

The response to this is quick and amazing. I am taken to meet a German pastor who is in the airport seeking news from Biafra.

"Ah." He says. "You have just come from Biafra?"

"Yes" is my brief response.

"But you sound as if you are British. Why are you travelling on the Swedish plane?"

I repeat my story to him and he asks me for more details as to where the Swedish Churches will be sending me.

"I am heading back eventually to be with my parents in Scotland."

"So where is the nearest Scottish airport to home?"

"Glasgow," I reply.

After this short conversation, he asks me to wait for a few moments, and when he returns he proffers me a plane ticket to Glasgow via London. This makes good sense to me, rather than having to continue my journey to Sweden. I am overwhelmed by his thoughtfulness and kindness. Such unexpected kindness from a total stranger! We then discuss my further travel plans and he discovers that to reach my parents' home it will cost perhaps another £5. He pulls some notes from his pocket and hands me £5 sterling. It's strange, but accepting the plane ticket feels so much easier than accepting the cash. I am embarrassed about accepting cash and it feels unsettling to be financially dependent on a complete stranger—almost as if I am begging for the money, a dependency on others which sits uncomfortably with me. I am starting to rediscover a strong desire to be independent, but this does not seem like the appropriate opportunity to act on it. I thank him for his kindness and support and take the money, but he stays to chat with me until the departure time of the London plane is confirmed on the information board.

Eventually, we are boarding the plane which will take us on the next stage of our journey, home to Scotland and back to the west coast where I was raised. The journey to London is smooth and uncomplicated, and our transfer to the Glasgow flight is straight-forward. As we settle into our seats for this stage of the journey, Ngozi starts to cry. She seems upset but I don't know what is wrong, as she cries and cries. She's maybe crying with hunger. I have powdered milk with me but the hostesses won't re-constitute it until we are in the air. I am seated beside a young gentleman, and I keep thinking about how annoyed he must be with all the noise and fuss around a baby! However, when we are finally airborne and Ngozi is fed and settled, I apologise to my neighbour for all the noise and distractions. He is kind enough to accept my apology and begins talking to me asking:

"How old is your daughter?

"She's three months," I reply hesitantly.

"She's beautiful," he continues. "I have a two year old daughter, and seeing your child reminds me of when my own daughter was born. Time flies so quickly and they grow up so fast; it's important to enjoy every minute you can with them while they are still young. Are you travelling far? My home is in Paisley, a short distance from the airport, and my car will be there for me to pick up," he continues, and again I start to feel wary of where this conversation is going. I feel a vulnerability around men whom I don't really know. He has told me his name is Sam, but I still see him as a stranger.

"I'm travelling down the coast to my parents' home." is my minimal response.

The airhostesses appear for the second time with drinks and sandwiches but I waive them aside again.

"Don't you want something to eat?" asks Sam. "You haven't eaten anything you've been offered, and the food is really nice."

"I realise that, but it looks so rich to me that I don't want to risk it. It's a long time since I saw food like that, and the quantities seem enormous. I'm not really very hungry."

As we are approaching Glasgow airport, an announcement comes over the intercom informing us that the plane is behind schedule and will be late in touching down. My heart immediately starts to beat fast, anticipating problems again, but I say nothing. It is still daylight, but I fear there will be no connections for me to reach Sandbank that evening. Sam now tells me the delay is making his return home easier as the roads will be quieter for him to drive on. Recognising that I may have a problem he suggests I accompany him to his home for an overnight. That familiar feeling rushes back: *can I trust him?* But I need help of some sort. So I suggest,

"When we have landed, if you first phone your wife and she is agreeable, and if I also have a quick word with her, *then* we can all travel together. You just can't arrive home with a strange woman and her child and expect your wife simply to accept it."

Having come off the plane, I hear him make the call and the response is positive. He hands me the phone and after speaking briefly with his wife I begin to feel a lot calmer. When we do arrive at his home his wife and daughter greet us enthusiastically. This is Scottish hospitality at its best. How can I describe it? Mary, his wife, recognises the limited "luggage" I have but doesn't comment on the sewing machine. She takes me into their daughter's bedroom and brings a suitcase with her, opens it and begins to take clothes from her daughter's chest of drawers.

"Look at all these lovely baby clothes that we were given when Dorothy was born and we have never used any of them. People are too generous. *You* must have them for Ngozi."

She fills the suitcase with a wide range of lovely infant clothing, including cosy hooded jackets, and then goes to find some warm clothes for me (we are about the same build). I am in floods of tears with gratitude. Later, after a meal, Mary is still curious about the sewing machine which has survived this tortuous journey with me, and I find myself telling her about the refugee camps, the desperate plight of the starving children, and what I was able to do to help in a small way. This helps to clarify the presence of the sewing machine. I sleep well that night, and the next morning Ngozi and I bid farewell to our hosts before continuing our journey to my parents' home. I am apprehensive about my parent's reaction to my impending return. I had made my defiant move but am coming home again, now with a child who needs her extended family. Given my African experiences, life can never be the same again, but Sandbank is familiar and will be comforting.

I alert my parents via neighbours who have a phone to the fact that we are back and heading home, but can't give any definitive details as to timings. Sam drives us to the railway station in Glasgow. I'm clutching my precious five pound note, and so am able to purchase the train ticket from Glasgow to Gourock. From Gourock we cross the River Clyde by ferry to Dunoon and then take a taxi home, arriving in the early evening. My father tells me he has come to the pier to meet every boat arriving during the day but finally gave up just before the last one, which was the very one we were actually travelling on.

What a reception we experience. My parents' relief that I am alive is tangible. It is September 1st, exactly three months since Ngozi was born, and how they embrace and love my little daughter. How concerned they are to see my weight loss, but ultimately we are actually back at home with them, and their tears and hugs are proof of their immense relief. There is no reference to their earlier recriminations about my marriage. They do not ask about Sennen, so I am uncertain whether they have changed their attitude about black people, and I decide not to ask. Motherhood is beginning to feel good, and the safe home environment is finally allowing me to fully relax. Campbell, my older brother is working in England, Ian is married, living nearby in Sandbank but planning to emigrate to the U.S.A. Angus, the youngest has served his apprenticeship as an electrician and is working in Glasgow.

Later, I learn that Mum had sent me parcels at various times after Ngozi was born. Missionary contacts had allowed me to send the news back to my parents when she was born. Mother's parcels contained baby products and essentials as well as clothing for all of us. I am sad to have to tell her that not one of her parcels ever reached me. I suspect that baby powder may have been mistaken for dried milk or even drugs, as Mum had removed the powder from the tins and re-packaged it in small plastic bags to reduce the weight. All the other items she included would have been invaluable in themselves, either to be used or sold on the black market. My father expresses his anger when I talk about the terror we felt during many air raids and he realises that these raids which were threatening Sennen, me and later Ngozi, were being partly financed by the UK government via his personal income tax payments—a real political irony.

Life as a single parent is now my reality. I'm married but there are four thousand miles separating me from my husband. It will be difficult to make any contact with Sennen unless I find someone who is planning to travel to Biafra, so I just wait to see how things may shape up. My parents are happy to support me in the short term, and help me to work out what I can do about the future. Mum's first task is to feed me up and help me renew my strength, but all I can face after years of starvation are small amounts of very basic food. My first request is for a simple shepherd's pie or mince and tatties. I'm also desperate to sample Mum's Scotch pancakes and scones again. It's a long, long time since I tasted such traditional Scottish food and I am gradually able to increase the size of my servings and begin to eat a properly varied diet.

My parents are so supportive and helpful - not questioning too much, but willing to listen when I want to talk about my experiences. I share with them the incident before the war when I attended a funeral with Sennen.

"One of the workmen at the power station has died in an accident, and it is necessary for his body to be returned to his ancestral village. Sennen thinks a native burial will be interesting for me to witness and so we both plan to attend. Many of the workman's colleagues are attending, so an open back lorry is arranged for them to travel in along with the body, and we follow in our own car. On reaching the village, the body is returned to the family and there are rites of passage to be performed. I take a back seat in all of this as I am a woman and not from the village. What I do recall is the firing of guns into the air in order to deter and chase away any evil spirits, to prevent them from harassing the family. The body will be buried close by, joining the ancestors who will jointly provide good protection for the family. Feasting will follow the interment but we do not remain for that. When, eventually, we do leave, Sennen again drives behind the lorry carrying his workmen. We drive in convoy like this for around twenty miles, along a good two lane straight tarred road. There is typical heavy growth on both sides of the road, and with no warning whatsoever a man on a bike rides out of the bush and straight into the path of our car. Sennen tries to avert a collision, but unfortunately, we hit the cyclist. He lands on the windscreen and shards of glass are peppered over us; the cyclist and car both end up in the ditch. We sat stunned for a few seconds, by which time natives are emerging from the bush. The driver of the lorry ahead of us has seen what has happened and has stopped. As we emerge from the car Sennen shouts at me,

"RUN, run for your life." and I take off up the road in bare feet. The men from the bush start throwing rocks at the car, and then one remembers there was a white woman in the car and comes after me. He catches up with me and is joined by other men. They grab me by the wrists and start to pull me into the bush. I'm terrified, imagining that I am probably heading for the missionary pot. I try speaking in Igbo to them.

"Ogene?" (What is it?) I ask. "Abum Igbo." (I am an Igbo) I cry. "Biko, biko." (Please, please.)

It momentarily startles them that I am speaking Igbo, but they continue to pull me closer and closer towards the bushes. The men in the lorry have also appeared on the scene, and they obviously want to rescue me, but can't quite decide how to manhandle their boss's wife. They decide to grasp me round the waist and pull against the others.

Out of nowhere in the middle of this struggle a police jeep arrives on the scene, and seeing a white woman in the middle of a melee they stop to investigate. The natives immediately evaporate into the bush and my life is saved. Phew, what an experience. The jeep is headed towards the scene of the accident, and they take me with them in their vehicle. They don't stop as we pass our car in the ditch, and I get a quick glimpse of Sennen, standing by the car, his head in his hands. Having been told I live in Oji River, the police agree to deliver me home. As we approach the village we are met by a crocodile of wailing women, heading back along the road to where we have come from. News has reached the power station concerning an accident and the wives are assuming the lorry is involved and their husbands are possibly all dead.

Stopping, we reassure them that all is well with the men on the lorry, but I am sensing that all is not well with

Sennen. How can it be if he has just killed a local man? In the end, a tow truck from the power station is sent to pull the car out of the ditch. It proves to be drivable in spite of the big dents in the bodywork and broken back and front windscreens. The injured man is not dead but apparently very drunk, so he is taken to the nearest hospital for a check on his injuries. Sennen eventually arrives back home just before midnight." Following this tale, my father's only cryptic comment is:

"And you say you want to go back to that country?" I can only smile.

I push Ngozi everywhere in her pram and talk to her about everything. The pram is a gift from my father. As we walk I also meditate and give thanks for so many things: The gift of a child, a safe return to Sandbank, a caring and supportive family, the many strangers I encountered along the way - some of whom I will never see again - and others like Sam and Mary who will remain friends. There is so much I am grateful for.

"Ngozi, see the gulls looking for fish in the water. That's where Grampa taught me to swim out there in the loch, and the day I first floated I nearly drowned with excitement. It was such a big event in my life. Maybe when you are a big girl I can teach you to swim out there too."

A little further along the road,

"Look at the lovely colours of the autumn trees!" I say, pointing to the birches and the sycamores, "These leaves are yellow, the ones over there are orange, and look at the lovely red berries on the rowan tree. The birds will like to eat these."

The autumn sun is reflecting off the silver bark of the birch trees, and we pause to enjoy the wonderful light display which creates a heartfelt sense of the wonder and the beauty of nature. Then I pick up a sycamore seed from the ground and throw it into the air. Ngozi squeals in delight as it twists its way back to earth and wants to do it herself.

"This is where Mummy used to camp when she was a Girl Guide," I tell her as we walk around the clearing in the woodland of the local estate.

And so the memories flow as I rediscover old haunts, and visit once-familiar places. Realising the changing of the seasons also begins to heal my hurt, as emotionally— and physically—I am returning to where life is more relaxed and pleasant, compared to my recent sequence of traumas and escapes. One of the routines I establish is to walk the two miles from home to the boatyard where my father works, meeting up with him at the end of his working day. Then we three walk back home together. Dad particularly enjoys stopping and sharing along the way in the interaction of others with Ngozi, and so the return trip takes twice as long as the original. Mum is becoming used to preparing a later evening meal. One evening at home Dad seems a bit pensive:

"Is there something wrong? Are you worrying about something?" I ask.

"Well, there was an incident at work today, and maybe it's better if you don't come along to the boatyard to meet me anymore."

"What! What happened that I can't simply walk to the boat yard and catch up with you after work? What exactly was this 'incident'?"

"I got involved in a discussion with the lads about mixed race marriages, and although I was defending your situation vociferously I was not supported by anyone else apart from David Smith. As tempers flared I backed off, but David continued to argue and eventually ended up in a fist fight with Campbell Munro. The place was in an uproar and the managers even came down from the office to find out what was going on. So maybe it's better not to come to the boat yard again."

"Prejudice is horrible, and the more so involving an innocent child! I don't want to be causing you trouble at work, so for your sake, I will do as you ask. Left to me, I would face up to those horrible workmates of yours, but on this occasion, I too will back down."

"I'm so sorry about this, but thanks for the support anyway."

Chapter Ten

Our Time in Glasgow

At home, conversations are beginning to revolve around what I am going to do, and whether or not I will remain in Sandbank and find local work. Eventually, I decided that I will return to Glasgow and complete the master's degree which I had previously taken only to diploma level. I investigate funding opportunities and discover that a generous grant can be made available to me as a mature student. So I take a trip to Glasgow and submit my application. I also visit the family with whom I had previously lodged as a student, and they offer me suitable accommodation including facilities for Ngozi. Next stop is the benefits office to register for family allowance and housing benefit. As I sit waiting my turn I am amazed at the information the other claimants offer me. They tell me about all the ways round the system and what ALL my entitlements could be. *So this is what the single parent/benefit community is all about*, I say to myself as I discover what financial support is available, and under what circumstances. My determination, however, is to be as self-reliant as possible, and although I appreciate the information I will only be accessing what I am legitimately entitled to claim.

After two months at home with my parents, I'm now in better health and my weight is returning to where it should be. It is time for me to move to Glasgow with Ngozi and begin our new life there. My pre-arranged accommodation consisting of one room with two alcoves is more than adequate. One alcove is where Ngozi will sleep in her pram; the other contains a cooker and a sink. The room itself is furnished as a bed-sit and the shared bathroom is outside on the landing. Everything we need is here. My landlords are Polish and they tell me they met and married in a concentration camp during the Second World War, so we are able to have a little understanding of each other's life experiences. They encourage me to write about my experiences and submit a short story to the Reader's Digest which offers a money prize for published articles. I am unsuccessful, but I retain my short script for the future as Ngozi may be interested in reading it.

Sennen and I have now been apart for a couple of months without any contact, so we don't know what is happening to each other. I am attending a local church where several people with young children quickly become close supportive friends. Many Scottish churches are raising funds specifically to support the war victims in

Biafra, and I am approached about my willingness to speak at meetings regarding my experiences of the war. I see this as a practical way of acknowledging my personal gratitude and also assuring donors of the many diverse ways in which both their money and the work of medical personnel are helping to make a difference. So I agree to do this.

I then attend various church meetings, taking Ngozi with me, explaining that although she is healthy now, we endured such dramas initially in keeping her alive. I also tell how difficult and heart-breaking it was for me to be out anywhere with her, and for local mums carrying emaciated infants to stop and want to greet us with broad smiles and to fondle Ngozi in a loving way. That was very hard for me as the comparisons between the infants were so odious.

By good fortune, the church becomes the conduit through which I am occasionally able to have letters delivered to Sennen via missionary contacts. I report to him on our new lifestyle, where I am staying, what I am doing and how I am coping. I do not tell him of the hours I trudge the streets feeling so lonely, simply wanting to be among people, be away from our lodgings and give Ngozi some fresh air. I don't mention the abuse I experience as a mother with a mixed race child, or how terrified I am when a car passing me simply back-fires. That sound is so like a gunshot, and so very close to me that my heart leaps every time it happens, and momentarily I look for shelter, before remembering where I am. Sennen on the other hand, when his hand delivered letters do manage to reach me, dare not give me any news as to his whereabouts or what he is doing in case his mail is intercepted and he is inadvertently revealing important information that could be useful to the enemy. He simply thanks me for my news and tells me he is well. At least this tells me he is still alive.

The miles of city streets that I trail with the pram take me to parts of the city I have never previously visited. In one such area, I find a small shop selling remnant material at a fair price and I buy some to make dresses for Ngozi as she grows. Now my sewing machine is coming into its own. I also come across a section of the Forth and Clyde Canal which I did not realise ran through one of the suburbs of the city where we walk. We stop and watch the boats making their way through the locks and I long for the carefree easy life they seem to symbolise. There is loneliness and sadness deep inside of me which friends and family are somehow unable to touch and I can't understand or explain it. I also haunt the various public parks, of which there are many in Glasgow. Victoria Park is within easy walking distance, and it is here that I re-discover the Fossil Grove where there are specimens of fossilised trees—geological remnants from three hundred million years ago, and this revives my former interest in geology. I smile and think again of the fossils from Somerset in England and from the Campsie Fells around Glasgow, all lying abandoned in Biafra, unrecognised and unloved!

When my studies begin at the university in mid-September Ngozi is now four months old and I enrol her in the local council day nursery. The service is free and Ngozi quickly becomes a favourite with the staff. I am surprised at just how supportive the nursery is. When I drop her off in the morning, she is, of course, wearing terry towelling nappies. When I collect her again later in the day, she has been fed, rested, changed into nursery supplied nappies, and then for going home she is dressed once more in her own clean and laundered nappies. She appears to be well settled and enjoying her nursery experience. For my part, I could not be more delighted with it.

I make new friends in class, some of whom are mature students like me. One such student, Jim, who is married with three children, becomes an especially supportive friend. Sometimes after classes, we go and collect Ngozi from the nursery and Jim drives us to a park where we walk and talk together. Like me, he is conscious of Ngozi's need for exercise and stimulation, so we enjoy introducing her to the swings and other available play equipment in the park that is suitable for her use. Eventually, I receive an invitation to visit Jim's family for a weekend and I look forward to meeting his wife and children. We spend a wonderful, relaxing and sociable weekend together, and I am happy for Jim's wife to get to know me well and have no fears regarding my friendship as a single woman with her husband—and now also with her. Their three daughters take great delight in looking after Ngozi and playing with her. She could almost be a member of their family as age-wise she fits comfortably behind the others.

Another friendship which I develop is with a Glaswegian called Sadie. We spend a lot of time together in class and become good friends. She is fascinated that I brought a sewing machine out of a war zone but is impressed that I have dressmaking skills. She sees some of the clothes I have made for Ngozi, and also for myself.

"Evelyn, do you think you could make a couple of summer dresses for me if I pay you?

"Of course I can. Bring me the pattern and the material you want, and I can sew in the evenings when Ngozi is asleep."

This works out well. Sadie is delighted with the dresses, and I am happy to add a little bit to my bank account. It has definitely been worthwhile bringing this machine back with me.

I have not been able to receive any really significant contact from Sennen, and have no idea what he may be doing until one day towards the end of my studies I am visited by a nun from the local Catholic Church.

"Greetings from Biafra," she announces.

"What is this about? Are you coming from Biafra and why do you think I have links with Biafra?"

"No, I have not come from there, but may I come in so that we can talk in private?"

I invite her in to my bedsit and find a chair for her to sit on.

"Now, please tell me what is going on." She comes straight to the point.

"I have very good news for you and your child. I believe she is called Ngozi? I have some money for you, a cheque for five hundred pounds no less." *Wow! That's close to a full year's salary as a teacher.*

"Why are you giving me this? Where has it come from?"

"Your husband is well and he has been negotiating with sisters from the hospital in Owerri where Ngozi was born. He reached an agreement with them and passed the equivalent of five hundred pounds to them on the understanding that the corresponding amount would be given to you, here in Scotland. He also made a generous donation to the hospital at the same time."

She hands me the cheque. I jump from my seat and hug her.

"Sister, bless you. How can I thank you? I am thrilled at what you have arranged. It's a real fortune to me in my circumstances. Let me tell you what this 'fortune' makes possible. I am shortly coming to the end of my current studies and when that occurs my student grant will run out. There's no way I want to be dependent on social services' handouts. Potentially I can now arrange a mortgage on a small flat somewhere in this area, and I will feel so much more settled and independent. Thank you so much. Now let's have a cup of tea and together celebrate my windfall."

My visitor is delighted that her mission is successfully accomplished and she can sense my joy in the situation. When she leaves I sit down again looking at the cheque and feel amazed that as one door begins to close another door always seems to open. I start imagining the possibilities that are now available to me and I waste no time discussing my windfall with church friends and discover that the husband of one of them is a solicitor specialising in residential sales. He suggests I delay until closer to my graduation following which I will undoubtedly be able to secure a well-paid job.

"When you have a job offer, that will be the time to put a large deposit on a property, have funds remaining, and pay the mortgage from a portion of your earnings. That way you will be financially secure with no questions about your ability to manage the necessary cash flow."

I agree this is good advice but I am impatient to buy a flat and so shortly before I complete my studies I move from rental to home ownership, courtesy of Sennen. I purchase a third storey one bedroom flat in a tenement building in Partick. It is number thirteen but I am not superstitious. My new flat has a kitchen/dining area, one bedroom, a sitting room with a walk-in cupboard and a bathroom. What more do I need? Oh! I am forgetting about furniture: a bed, a table, dining chairs, a suite. I will also need to furnish the kitchen. Initially while having the keys to the flat, I continue to lodge in my rented room while I furnish the flat. Once more the kind people of Sandbank, via my parents' requests, make provision for me by donating cooking equipment, dishes, and cutlery. As to the furniture, I don't reckon I need much before moving in. Ngozi will continue to sleep in her pram initially, and a bed settee will double up as a seating /sleeping arrangement for me. I scour the second hand shops and find what I need, have my bed settee delivered and I can now move in, taking time to acquire all the other items as and when I can.

Church friends who have been following my progress since agreeing to buy the flat are delighted for me, and I am now able to invite them to see me "at home" and share a cup of tea. This begins to feel slightly closer to normality. One friend visits with her young daughter and I'm proudly giving them the show-round when in the bedroom where Ngozi sleeps, the youngster gasps in concern and announces,

"But, Mum there aren't any carpets in the bedroom!"

My friend is embarrassed but I pass it off as a natural reaction from the youngster and I am not offended. I hear later, that when they leave the flat her daughter will just not let the matter drop, and so the next time I see them is when they ring the doorbell and bring me a small carpet!

The delight of the youngster is palpable. She is grinning from ear to ear and can't wait to come in. She is further delighted when I suggest:

"Would you like to decide where and how your carpet should be laid?"

It seems as if life is no sooner stabilising when new problems arise. I would like to have good contact with my parents (they still don't have a telephone) but the journey between Glasgow and Sandbank requires four separate forms of public transport and the timings do not always coincide with each other for the convenience of the travelling public. Having made this journey several times, heaving a pram on and off public transport, I decide I have had enough. I discuss the problem with my brothers, and Angus, my youngest brother makes a suggestion. He is working as an electrician in Glasgow and is able to lend me the money to buy a small car. The arrangement is that I will pay him back as and when I can. He knows he can trust me and so we search together and purchase a second-hand - but reliable - Morris minor for £100. I am now in a position to visit my parents on a regular basis. Life's problems have a way of eventually being solved, albeit one by one.

During the latter part of my studies, focussing on final exams and being intellectually challenged my thoughts are thus diverted temporarily from focussing on my status as a single parent with a husband several thousand miles away and minimal communication between us. For some time during the year, the senior psychology lecturer has been offering me extra individual meeting times, taking an apparent interest in my personal situation. As well as offering a mentoring service around my psychology studies he engages me in conversations about my personal lifestyle and how I currently spend my free time. He is very understanding and a good listener. He never offers solutions or advice; he simply listens and is empathetic towards me. I begin to realise the benefit of opening up honestly about all sorts of issues to a trusted listener, and so my "therapy"—though not being named as such—proves really helpful to me. I guess he has some awareness of managing symptoms of post-traumatic stress syndrome, although at the time I had never heard of the condition.

The war in Biafra continues to rage, and BBC news reports continue to comment on, and photograph refugee camp situations. For the first time ever, TV is showing images of children suffering from kwashiorkor and serious malnutrition in war zones overseas. My parents can scarcely believe that this is a true picture of what I experienced while there. Life continues in this vein for some time, and then I graduate with a good master's degree in education and psychology in the summer of 1970. I look for work, planning to do something in the field of research, and an opportunity comes my way—an offer of employment within the local council's research and development department. Under the auspices of "urban aid", I become involved in a project focussing on pre-school language development. I visit many nurseries and advise on reading habits and aural issues as well as oral communication sessions.

Some time later, I move on to a new piece of development work. This time I exercise my direct training skills, working internally with social work staff on issues of monetary decimalisation. The change from familiar sterling to a decimal currency which the government is introducing is seen as leaving many people in a quandary, panicking about the February 1971 changeover date, and how to deal with it when it finally arrives. It reminds me of the time in Nigeria when driving was changed from the left hand side of the road to the right hand side. For several weeks in the lead up to that change, the radio was broadcasting the information with jingles, and the date of its implementation was repeatedly being reinforced. When the change came into force many drivers stayed off the roads for several days until things began to settle down. I wonder how long it will take in Scotland to embed the decimal currency changes which are being implemented. To start the information process locally, I am allocated groups of social workers whom I train to pass on the required knowledge about the new coins to their individual elderly clients. Yet another project involves me visiting pensioners in high rise buildings across the city. I discuss finances with them and help each one to sort out a reasonable budget which will keep them free from debt. I find this a particularly rewarding piece of work as I am warmly welcomed by the older people, to whom I am just a youngster, but I come bringing them such helpful and useful information. I can't begin to count the number of cups of tea I am offered during those visits. Glasgow people do have a wonderful reputation for friendliness. On opening the door to me I was invariably invited, "Come in and have a cup of tea then."

Working with social workers brings me into contact with many new acquaintances and I have grown particularly friendly with Amanda, a social worker of my own age. When we spend any free time together we talk and talk and talk. She often comes to my flat and we drink black coffee far into the night to keep ourselves awake while Ngozi sleeps on in the bedroom. Many evenings it's after midnight when Amanda eventually and reluctantly has to head for home as I have no spare accommodation available.

I am busy with all these interesting development projects when I receive a letter from Sennen. At first, I smile with delight and my heart races in anticipation of the good news he may be sending, but as I continue to read, my smile gradually disappears. He tells me the war is now over. Biafra surrendered in January 1971 and his life is so miserable compared to the wonderfully free and easy life I obviously have here in Glasgow. That may be his perception, but it certainly isn't mine. *Does he not remember the prejudice we experienced as students?* He then implores me to return immediately with Ngozi. How can I just drop everything and go? I can't—even if I wanted to! I have a job where I need to give in my notice before I can leave. I own a flat and a car, both of which I will need to deal with before I am free to go. I'm thoroughly confused and troubled by this sudden turn of events. I take time to think all this through, trying to sort out my feelings and consider how to reply.

Eventually, I sit down and write:

"Dear Sennen,

Thanks for your news and I'm so happy to hear from you now that things seem to be more settled. Hopefully, we will now be able to send and receive letters normally. It must be strange being back working at the power station again, and living in the same house. I'm glad the house wasn't damaged during the fighting. Things here, however, are not as you seem to think. Being a single parent still brings prejudice and contempt from many people, and the fact that our child is mixed race only adds to that, as no-one apart from friends is aware of my true circumstances. Certainly, there are Caribbean people aplenty in Glasgow, mainly working on the buses. There are numerous Chinese restaurants, and many of the corner shops are owned and run by Indians, but none of these people are in an inter-racial marriage. That's what is bringing me the problems. As you know I got a good degree when I went back to study and now I have a well- paid research position in the city. It would be really easy for you to come here now and secure a very good job in Scotland as well, and we have a secure, comfortable flat thanks to your earlier foresight and generosity. So what, I'm asking, is there to keep you in a post-war area of Nigeria, when you are already familiar with Glasgow? It seems a no-brainer that you should choose to return here to a city we both know so well, where we can build our lives back together again. Ngozi is doing well. She's healthy, happy and attends a day nursery while I am at work. Please, please, will you think about coming here? I'm sure there would be a senior position for you somewhere. Think seriously about it.

I look forward to hearing from you soon again.

Ever your loving wife (and daughter)

Evelyn"

A few more letters are exchanged with no sign of Sennen dropping his plea for me to return to Nigeria, and other correspondence also begins to arrive from some of his friends, insisting that I **must** return.

Ngozi is approaching her third birthday and is a bright precocious youngster. I wonder how such impending and dramatic changes in our lifestyle will affect her if and when we return to Nigeria. My head is muddled as I try to resolve this dilemma. *Should I / shouldn't I go back?* I decide to seek the opinion of others. On my next visit home I talk to my parents.

"I've just had a letter from Sennen who tells me things are settled again and he is back in his old job and former house. He's asking me to go back, although I would have a few things to sort out prior to going."

"Are you mad? We remember the story you told us about the funeral when you nearly lost your life, and that was in peace time. You've established a decent life for yourself and Ngozi in Glasgow, and although we know it's not always easy for you at least you are safe and can keep in touch with us through the regular visits you make. We would miss you both desperately. So please, no more talk of going back."

"I'll think about what you say, but at the end of the day I have a husband and Ngozi has a father in Nigeria. Would you want me to be held responsible for sabotaging both these relationships?"

"You do what you think you have to do, but please, please, *this time*, remember our advice to you."

I return to Glasgow more confused than ever. No pros

or cons have been discussed and I desperately want to keep my parents on side. My alternative strategy is to seek the advice of church friends. I talk to several individuals at various times. With each of them, I have a more reasoned exchange, but their underlying message is the same.

"Evelyn, you were married in the church and made your vows before God and witnesses. You need to consider whether you can break these vows with a clear conscience."

This seems less didactic than my parents' comments, but the decision, whichever way it goes, still ultimately rests with me. As the weeks pass I realise that if our marriage is to survive I must return as is being demanded of me, and so I begin to plan and make the necessary arrangements. First I give a month's obligatory notice at work. I am really sad to be leaving but also surprised to realise that so many of my colleagues are expressing their regret with my decision and also openly disagree with me about it. Next, I consider options regarding our flat. It has risen in value and I could sell. Alternatively, I could try to find a tenant and rent it. I talk to my friend Jim about this and he refers me to his brother-in-law who is a solicitor dealing with rentals. Then, totally unexpectedly, Amanda comes to the rescue. She wants to move away from living with her parents and rent a flat. We have talked endlessly about my plans and she now approaches me offering to become my trusted tenant. I chat about this possible arrangement with the solicitor and he agrees to draw up the contractual arrangements for me. The flat will be single occupancy, with no pets allowed. The income from the rental is to be transferred to my parents. The loan in respect of the car has already been repaid to my brother, so no problem there, and a neighbour, upon hearing of my impending departure, offers to buy my car for a reasonable sum. I prepare the flat for Amanda and lock all our personal belongings in the walk-in cupboard in the sitting room. *Did I have a premonition that I would return someday and require all these things like winter clothing, books, and white goods?* The flat is being left in a fully furnished state for my new tenant and as we are finally leaving, she is simultaneously moving in, so we are able to exchange our fond farewells.

Chapter Eleven

A Reluctant Return to Nigeria

This time I fly with Ngozi to Lagos in the late spring of 1971. Sennen knows our flight plans and timings. He has indicated that he is preparing to meet us when we arrive. We fly first with KLM to Amsterdam where we endure a long wait before joining the direct flight to Lagos. The facilities at Amsterdam airport are pretty amazing. They provide all sorts of entertainment for young children like Ngozi and so she is well occupied, while I do my usual thing and read a book. I am conscious that we are dressed according to cool spring weather, and when we arrive in Nigeria it will be very much hotter. Moving from Scotland to the tropics requires adapting to immense temperature differences. I'm used to Scotland's summer temperature in July being perhaps 15°c – 17°c whereas in Nigeria the hottest month is around 28°c, and being tropical there is only a small variation in the temperature between the hottest and the coolest months. There are only two seasons rather than four: a wet season from April to October and a dry season from November to March, and during the rainy season the humidity is unbearable. Four or five cold showers a day can be the norm, it's so uncomfortable.

We are therefore dressed in layers of clothing which I plan to remove gradually according to the changes in temperature in Lagos. We eventually board the plane for Lagos, and six hours later we prepare to touch down in Nigeria. I meet fierce resistance from Ngozi when I try to exchange her warm woollen tights for cotton ankle socks, so I leave her as she is. As we descend from the air-conditioned comfort of the plane the heat hits us like a blast from an oven. Sweat begins to trickle down our faces, and Ngozi will still not remove her tights or her cardigan. We pass through arrivals, collect our luggage and wait in the lounge for Sennen. We wait and we wait and we wait. Where is he? Without mobile phones, there is no way of contacting each other. Staff approach me to find out why we are waiting for such a long time. I explain the problem to them and they offer to contact the British Embassy on my behalf. I agree to this and after some time an official arrives and we discuss the situation. "What's the problem here, then? I understand your husband was meant to be meeting you."

"Yes, he was. He knew our travel plans and was going to meet us here, which is why I have remained where he can find me. I don't know what's happened to him and I'm becoming anxious. I have no contacts in Lagos who can help me out."

"This is precisely where the Embassy can step in and resolve your dilemma. We can look after you, provide emergency accommodation as required, and we will try and make contact with your husband. How does that sound to you?"

This seems an eminently sensible solution and at least we will not be at the mercy of the touts and beggars who frequent places like airports, pestering individuals—especially foreigners—in the hope of being given money. So we accept the arrangements for an overnight; the following day Sennen arrives at the Embassy and we are able to set off on the familiar journey to Oji River and the power station where Sennen has been re-instated to his former post. Maybe the fact that he never officially "joined" the resistance movement has allowed him to be reasonably acceptable to the new Nigerian administration.

I'm annoyed that Sennen offers no reason for his non-appearance when he definitely knew our arrival time, but I recall the many occasions in the past when no reasons were given to me when I queried matters, and so I remain silent. Ngozi is curious about this new man in her life: "Is this my Daddy?" she asks, and I realise that our return to Africa may be far from straightforward. As far as Ngozi is concerned, the main men in her life so far have been my younger brother Angus and her grandfather in Sandbank. Angus, who has been a regular visitor to the flat, has on occasion had to *try* to discipline her for being cheeky or not doing what she was asked to do. This was a good supporting role to mine. Now it will be her father's turn – or so I thought.

Back in a familiar home, I begin the task of settling Ngozi into this her new environment. Our housemaid Charity has returned to live with us, and she now has a colleague, Beatrice, another young village girl whose main responsibility is going to be to look after Ngozi.

Ngozi is confused by all the changes expected of her, the main one being that there is a floor mat for her to sleep on beside Beatrice who is also using a sleeping mat.

"This won't do, Sennen, Ngozi is used to sleeping on a proper mattress in her pram or in a bed," I say to her father.

"But this is how our children sleep. Don't worry, Beatrice will be responsible for her overnight, and will take good care of her."

"Maybe so, but I don't think you understand. This kind of change for Ngozi is massive. Please try and find her a proper bed." I plead.

This is the start of much confusion around Ngozi's change of cultures. The food is also unfamiliar to her. No more Krispies for breakfast. No more boiled eggs and toasted soldiers to dip. No more fresh milk to drink. It's very hard for her and she can't be expected to understand. There are other anomalies too. She complains to me,

"Mummy, I'm cold. There are no fires in our new house, and there's no TV. Why can't I watch Dugald or Bambi?"

I just give her a hug and tell her that we can make our own fun, and Beatrice will teach her some new games. With her third birthday fast approaching I decided to celebrate by simply baking a traditional birthday cake and decorating it with three candles. She will see this as more normal and we will share it with Beatrice and Charity. I am pleasantly surprised to realise that Ngozi is quickly beginning to speak a few words of Igbo, courtesy of Beatrice's poor English, but as Ngozi's English vocabulary continues to develop there will undoubtedly be mutual cross-learning taking place.

The war now being over, schools are back in action and so my teaching job picks up again in the same school as before. I'm back in my former routine, teaching my old subjects of geography, elementary French and Nigerian history. The boys who know me welcome me back, but I am sad to notice the number of missing students. I learn that many of the older boys had joined the resistance to fight for Biafra, and in so doing have lost their lives.

At home, things are not working out well. Ngozi continues to be upset by all the unfamiliarity of her daily life. She no longer goes to a nursery but spends the entire day at home with the two girls unless she comes with me when shopping. I regularly borrow the car to do a weekly shop in Enugu with her and Beatrice, and on the way, we have to pass several security road checks. At each checkpoint, we are stopped. Armed soldiers ask me to step outside and sometimes I have to go with them into their small hut to be questioned. They are, of course, Nigerian soldiers now "occupying" what was formerly Biafra. It seems they are suspicious of a white woman in the area so soon after the war. I'm never quite sure whether using my Igbo will help or hinder the situation. These security checks invariably pass without incident, but on returning to the car where Ngozi is waiting; she always asks me the same question,

"Mummy, are the soldiers going to shoot you?"

"No, no. It's ok. They are only talking to me."

How can I be sure that this is reassuring to a three year old while also hiding my general apprehensions and frustration from her?

Sennen does not talk about any of his war experiences, so I am left to wonder. Apart from the mental suffering caused by our enforced separation when I left with Ngozi, albeit by mutual agreement, I do wonder about his later experiences as he was loosely connected to the Biafran military. However, he adamantly refuses to share anything about that period of time with me. So I am left to cope in a marriage where we no longer share deep feelings with one another or have any conversations about the past. Work appears to be his only pre-occupation. On the other hand, the home, the house-girls and Ngozi would appear to be my side of an unspoken agreement regarding distinct and separate responsibilities. In addition, I have my teaching duties. The focus of any conversations we do have revolves around investments which Sennen is considering making. He is planning to invest in the residential property market and is also considering the stock market. I knew nothing about such matters in Scotland, never mind being expected to know here in Nigeria. I become irritated by the repeated requests for me to make the decision about particular specific investments. I don't know enough, nor am I really interested, so how can I make a rational decision? I also resist this pressure as I suspect it is not a woman's place to take the lead and confirm the move. Culturally I'm uncertain about the whole thing. I smile ironically to myself as I think that should it all go belly-up, then the blame will most certainly be mine if the original advice were to be mine. On all these counts I refuse to make any decision and this angers Sennen.

Here I am again at the mercy of cross-cultural misunderstandings and confusion. I often wonder if the current changes in Sennen's behaviour are linked to his war-time experience. *Has it been so awful that he can't face talking about it? Is he losing confidence and becoming dependent on me for so many things? Does he have the money to cover the many varied investments he talks about? Does he still love me?*

I have no answer to any of this, and if he is suffering from post-traumatic stress, then I am not best placed to support him or even to suggest that it may be part of the issue between us. I try to meet all the expectations and duties required of me, but I realise that the love between us has gradually dissipated since my return. Then we have a domestic catastrophe. I am busy tidying our personal belongings in the bedroom and I inadvertently knock Sennen's electric razor onto the hard tiled floor. The plastic casing breaks and I am surprised at my own reaction. My stomach tightens, beads of sweat appear on my forehead and I begin to dread the moment I will have to admit to what I've done. The razor is a valued possession and I fear Sennen will react with fury at my carelessness. When he returns from work in the evening, we have our meal in silence as usual. When I can no longer delay my confession I fetch the shattered remnants, hold them in my hand I try to explain what has happened. He does not reply. Suddenly he lashes out and without a word strikes me really forcibly across my bare upper arm.

Ouch. That was uncalled for. That was actually an assault! I face him stoically, not wanting him to realise how sore he is making me feel both physically and emotionally. *Shades of sibling interactions return to my thoughts. I can get through this, but he won't know how.* He turns away, calmly changing the subject and instructs me,

"You are remembering that we are invited to join our neighbours tonight for a social evening and we *will* be going."

My upper arm is showing evidence of being struck hard—a red and blue weal appearing depicting four fingers. It is impossible to hide my injury and so I put on a brave face and attend our neighbours' social event. No-one says anything to me about the bruising on my arm, but I do see that people are noticing it. It makes for an uncomfortable evening of socialising for me, and I am constantly close to tears. The following day I cannot get the situation out of my mind. Breaking his razor was, after all, an accident. What am I to do? I wonder if this is typical Igbo behaviour between husband and wife, and I fear that having hit me once he will do it again. It's a massive decision to take, but I will not stay and risk further physical and emotional abuse. I resolve to leave and take Ngozi with me. I can recall the previous time when Sennen spoke about wives who leave an inter-racial marriage and how the children of that marriage are considered to be the property of the husband. I say nothing but begin to plan. *I have money in the bank in Enugu from my teaching post, enough to pay for a single journey back to Scotland. There are flights from Enugu to Lagos, so that will work.* Rebellious, independent and feeling resourceful, my plans begin to take shape. We have been back in Nigeria a mere five months. I wait for a day when Sennen is at work all day and I begin to put my plan into operation by talking to Ngozi,

"How would you like to go and visit Gran and Grampa back in Scotland?"

She responds enthusiastically and so I pack a small bag

with nightwear and underwear and we set off immediately.
I leave no note. I simply go.

Chapter Twelve

Leaving Nigeria - AGAIN

We walk the mile down into the valley and wait for the local bus. I am hoping that, to anyone seeing us, it looks like a shopping trip to the town. Walking a mile to the bus stop is not what an expatriate would normally be expected to do, but when needs must, unusual things can happen. The bus stop is not far from the power station and I am hoping that no-one who knows me sees me and reports to Sennen, thus scuppering my plans. When we board the bus and set off up the hill, I breathe a sigh of relief. We are on our way. Unfortunately, the bus does not make it to the top of the hill, breaking down at the roadside and forcing all the passengers to return to the departure point. We are back where we started. What will happen now? Fortunately, within half an hour of waiting, or in our case "hiding" in the bus shelter, we are able to board another bus and arrive finally in Enugu.

We make the trip to the bank and I lift an amount of money to cover the journey costs, allowing also for any unforeseen eventualities. It's just as well I do so, as when we go to the travel office to buy the plane tickets we discover that there are no current flights available. *Why are my plans always compromised like this?* I feel very vulnerable as we are not too far from home at this point, so I must think of an alternative plan. I decide to head for Lagos on a long distance coach; we should be able to do that without any problem except for one. The bus does not go as far as Lagos but will take us half way there, that is, to the crossing point on the River Niger. Well, better than going nowhere—or even worse, back to Oji River—so we make the journey, this time without incident. My plan is to pick up another bus which will complete the journey for us. At the staging point, we dismount and join the Lagos-bound bus. I pay for two seats as it is too hot for Ngozi to sit on my lap, and we will both be more comfortable seated side by side given the length of the journey to Lagos. As the bus begins to fill up I am approached by a woman:

"I would like to sit on the window seat beside you. Please take your child on your lap."

"I'm sorry, the seat's not available. I have paid for two seats because it is so hot and I don't want to put the child on my lap."

"Put the child on your lap."

"Sorry. I've already explained. Her seat is already paid for."

"PUT THE CHILD ON YOUR LAP."

The bus driver, becoming aware of this altercation, intervenes and announces he is going nowhere until we resolve the situation. He gives me my options. The simple way to resolve it is for me to put the child on my lap or leave the bus. I appear to have *no* option, and the argumentative woman has others agreeing with her, so I take my small bag, receive a refund on my fares and we dismount. I am beginning to feel that I attract trouble wherever I go! As we step down from the bus another young woman also steps down, and the bus is now free to depart. This other young woman is upset at the behaviour of her compatriots towards me and wants to help. "Do you want to go all the way to Lagos?" she asks.

"Yes. That is my plan, but it's already getting late and my daughter is tired. I'm exhausted by all the aggression I was subjected to on the bus."

"Can I make a proposal? I'm not travelling as far as Lagos, only as far as Benin City, so we could share a taxi to get there. I suggest you then go to the Rest House, the one that the expatriates use when travelling. You could overnight there and continue to Lagos tomorrow."

I wonder whether I can trust this stranger or not, but I want to be as far away as possible from Oji River as I fear being followed, found and returned. All things considered, it seems to make sense to accept this offer of help, and so I decided to run with it.

My taxi companion is so kind. In Benin, she instructs

the driver to take me to the Rest House, the small hotel she recommended, as she thinks I will find it acceptable. Yes, indeed I do find it comfortable and I am able to order food via room service for Ngozi and myself. I want to keep myself to myself as much as possible and avoid conversations with any strangers. I ask myself: *Am I becoming paranoid?* but decide it's more a matter of personal safety. *There is no way I will ever return to live with Sennen, neither here in Nigeria nor back in Scotland. For me, the matter is now a closed book.*

We have our meal and I settle Ngozi for the night. She seems unperturbed by the various adventures we have stumbled through in arriving here. I can't wait for the morning to come when we can be on our way again.

In the morning when I waken Ngozi to get her up and dressed I find that during the night she has wet her bed. This is the first time ever! My heart drops. Is this her reaction to what is going on? How can I tell, because I don't want to ask her or comment on the overnight "accident"? So we have our showers, get dressed and prepare to risk the public dining room for breakfast. I open the curtains and gasp with fright. Right outside our window is a company van bearing the ECN logo belonging to the company which employs Sennen. I almost give up in despair. My heart is working over-time, I'm close to tears, and my thoughts are in turmoil. What will happen if we have been traced and found? Now we will no longer be going anywhere near that dining room. We stay in our room *HIDING* from whoever is in that van. I hold my head in my hands. When I look back over the last seven years I feel my life has been a constant nightmare apart from a fairly brief early interlude. *Why did I ever allow myself to be seduced by such an emotionally unreliable character? Is this how post-war situations affect men?* The only good to come out of it is I now have a beautiful mixed race daughter whom I can care for in appropriate ways, who will eat normal food, has loving grandparents who will support us, and when the time comes will have a decent Scottish education.

I think back to my university days and to other students whose advances I rejected and wonder what might have been, but that is mere speculation. I know for a fact that some of these young men married other classmates of the time. I bring myself back to the present and start to curtain twitch, willing the van to be gone, and after an hour I finally spot it driving away. We venture in to the dining room and have our meal. For the first time in five months, Ngozi can enjoy her favourite Krispies for breakfast.

Now it's time for what I hope is going to be the last leg of our journey to Lagos airport. We board the long distance bus, I pay for two seats, and this time there is no problem. Ngozi is sitting in the window seat, her short legs straight out in front of her. The Nigerian gentleman across the passage way tries to strike up a conversation with me.

He comments on the "nice red sandals" my daughter is wearing. I simply nod and agree. Then he continues:

"Where did you buy these sandals?"

Is this an attempt to identify where we come from? I am definitely becoming paranoid, and decide that the best answer is just to mention Onitsha as it is a centralised shopping venue for many expatriates. He is delighted to hear this and continues,

"I am an importer, and these sandals are part of my trade. Onitsha is one of my very successful distribution centres. Thank you for purchasing them."

I sigh with relief and close my eyes. I reckon that if I appear to be sleeping I will not be disturbed by further questioning. One of the bus stops in Lagos is outside the Airport Hotel, so we dismount here and check in to the hotel. This gives me time to investigate the flight times from Lagos to Glasgow. I am so glad I had the foresight to lift a good amount of cash from the bank in Enugu, and trust there is enough as my fund is being rapidly depleted. We are not heading for Sandbank on this occasion as my parents have no idea of what has happened, or even that we are returning. My plan is to reach Glasgow and find out what is happening to Amanda and my flat. I expect that as a former close friend she will be willing to help me out at least for a short time. So we spend one night in the airport hotel, speaking to no-one other than staff, and at the appropriate time transfer from the hotel to the airport, where I purchase our tickets. Now my spirits are on the up, and I begin to relax. It's very hot and humid inside the airport lounge so I decided we should sit outside for comfort on one of the benches in the shade. I notice a number of armed security guards pacing around the building and runways. I have to remind myself that the country was at war up until fairly recently. We are sitting there in the shade for about a quarter of an hour when one of the guards approaches us. "*What now?*" I ask myself. The conversation goes something like this:

"Good morning Madam."

"Good morning."

"Is this your daughter?"

"Yes."

"You are travelling today?"

"Yes."

"Where are you travelling to?"

"London," I reply protectively if dishonestly. All my expectations of escaping are fast disappearing. My heart is in my boots. I give a sigh of resignation. So near and yet so far, is what I'm thinking. Then unexpectedly he says:

"Have a good journey," and walks away.

Phew! That was a close call. I realise that I will only begin to feel really safe when we are on that plane and it is off the runway and in the sky.

Chapter Thirteen

Welcome back to Scotland

Finally, we do reach London, transfer without problems and arrive in Glasgow complete with hand luggage. We left Oji River on Thursday morning and it's now Saturday afternoon. Our travels have taken three days and I am exhausted. We take a taxi to Lawrence Street, and Ngozi laughs with delight as she recognises where she used to live. I have my personal set of keys to hand, and we climb to the third storey of the building. I stare in disbelief. The storm doors are closed. This is not a good sign. When I try my keys in the lock they refuse to operate. Where is Amanda and what's going on? Where can I turn to for help? What other friends are around with whom I may be willing to share my current situation? Maybe the solicitor managing the rental situation has proper keys, but a phone call confirms his office is closed on Saturdays. That prompts an idea. I recall he is a relative of Jim so I will contact my friend, Jim, from student days and explain the closed office and wrong key set. That is what I do and he immediately suggests he will come to town, collect us and we can have a weekend with him, Jessie and the girls. When we meet up he tells me the girls can't wait to see Ngozi again. He is curious about the small amount of luggage I am carrying, so I revert to another untruth and explain our main luggage is "in one of the left luggage lockers at the railway station." I doubt if Jim actually believes me but like the true friend he is, he doesn't question this information. We enjoy the weekend with the family, and then on Monday morning we come back into Glasgow and head for the solicitor's office. Amanda, as I suspected, has indeed left the flat, reclaimed her deposit, deposited the new set of keys with the solicitor and disappeared. I am disappointed by her silence and when we finally get into the flat I find that there is damage to my furniture which looks as if a cat has been using the front of the bed settee as a scratching post. There are a few missing items also, but nothing that is essential. I'm glad I secured certain belongings in the locked cupboard when I was leaving. I am the only one holding that particular key and so it has remained undisturbed and unopened. Neighbours greet my return with pleasure, and they inform me that Amanda lost her keys and had to change the locks. They confirm the existence of a resident cat—specifically against the terms of her lease. They also tell me that Amanda's mother was staying there permanently with her—again contrary to the lease agreement. As our good friendship has been so grossly abused it's no surprise that I will not be planning to see her again.

Ngozi and I quickly settle back into a routine and I apply to the Education Department for a teaching post. I also enrol Ngozi in a local pre-school nursery, and I am delighted to find the service is again free. This time I am sufficiently solvent to invest in another small car, so I purchase a second-hand Volkswagen. Next, I send word to my parents and arrange to visit them. How will they respond this time? Yet again I have not followed their advice to me, and yet again matters did not turn out well for me. It feels like a case of "I told you not to do it, but you are so headstrong and independent, always doing things your own way. Now, look what's happened."

So I am apprehensive about my parents' reaction to my impending visit. I have made my defiant moves but am coming home permanently this time. Given my African experiences, life can never be the same again, but Sandbank is familiar and comforting. My African rebellion is totally and finally over. I have discovered a personal resilience I was previously unaware of, and motherhood has arrived, bringing with it immeasurable joy and hope for the future. I pray that I might receive a prodigal's welcome.

I steel myself for whatever reaction I will encounter on arrival. Mum greets me warmly, but her main concern is that my father is very unwell. He is suffering from chronic breathing problems and can no longer work.

Years of working in the boatyard's saw-mill with carcino-
genic hardwoods and no protective masks have damaged
his lungs. He is now virtually bed-bound and sleeps in the
downstairs bedroom of their council house, thus making
it easier for Mum to care for him. There are, therefore,
no recriminations, only pleasure that I am around at this
difficult time and available as a support to them. I begin
to visit regularly, and during summer visits I invite one of
Ngozi's friends, Alison, to come with us. This is the younger
sister of the girl who brought us a rug for the bedroom.
The journey takes us out of Glasgow, along the banks of
Loch Lomond and over the famous hill road known as
"The Rest and Be Thankful". This is a wonderfully scenic
route with hills, valleys, forests, and streams all around.
Sometimes we spot red deer on the hillsides and raptors
in the sky, eagle eyes waiting for the slightest movement
in the undergrowth. We establish a number of favourite
spots where we stop and picnic away from the official
picnic sites. This means we have just our own company,
and I regale the girls with fairy tales and adventure stories
to entertain them. We also search the burns for "gold" or
pyrites, which is usually referred to as fool's gold, and it
thrills the girls to find any small nuggets which they can
then show to Gran and Grampa. On one occasion while
exploring around our chosen picnic spot we come across a
single antler with several points which had been shed. The
girls are thrilled with this unexpected find, "Oh, Mummy,

do you think this belongs to Rudolph? What will he do with just one antler? He will look really funny." is the first comment.

"No, no. Rudolph will have dropped both his antlers, so there is another one around at a different place on the hillside. Next year he will just grow new ones."

"Was he in a fight and that's why they are broken?"

"Well sometimes reindeer do fight but that's not why this antler is here. It's not broken. Every year in the springtime it just happens that the antlers fall off, and then they grow new ones ready to fight if necessary in the autumn."

So we take the solitary antler with us. Perhaps I can sell it, or find a horn smith who can turn parts of it into useful items such as the handle for a shepherd's crook, a whistle from one of the tips, handles for cutlery, coat hooks, candle holders—the list is endless.

"Mummy, mummy, is that an eagle?" asks Ngozi, excitedly pointing overhead.

"No dear, it's only a crow, but if I do see an eagle I will stop again and let you watch it."

Reaching Sandbank, we have barely exchanged greetings with my parents before the girls are excitedly entertaining them with the story of our new finds.

Once the girls go outside to play, the conversation becomes more serious. My father's health is deteriorating fast. His breathing is much laboured and his colour is grey. On the assumption that he is not going to recover, my brother Ian who lives in America returns to visit Sandbank. This is likely the last time he will see Dad, so he is planning to stay for a month before returning to his own family in Loveland, Ohio. Angus is still around in the Glasgow area, and my dad sets the two of them a challenge. On previous visits to my flat, Dad has noticed things that I don't see regarding maintenance. He has a long conversation with the boys which results in him instructing them to rewire the flat completely and then to redecorate all the rooms. Wow! "Tradesmen" who are not going to charge me for a significant amount of professional work! I recall as a child that my father and the boys did all kinds of renovation work around the house at home, and when a tradesman was required, there was always a professional "friend" to help out.

Returning with me to Glasgow, my brothers take on the challenge, working in the evenings when Angus and I are home from work. Weekends produce a frenzy of activity— all hands on deck, so to speak. The work is well under way, but not yet complete when Ian announces it is time for him to return to the States, and after a final visit to Sandbank, he departs. By the time the work is eventually complete the flat is looking fresh and modern and has surely increased in value.

I want to thank my father for initiating all this, and when I next visit I realise he really is near to his end. Back in Glasgow, I think about arrangements in the event of his death. Church friends again to the rescue! I will be able to leave Ngozi in Glasgow with trusted friends and return to Sandbank on my own. This arrangement serves me well when my father dies a few weeks later as Angus and I can be at home and help with all the funeral arrangements. This is the first time I have experienced the loss of someone close, and I feel confused and upset. I recall the special relationship I had with my Dad throughout my earlier life, and as I reminisce about those days the tears begin to flow. I somehow make it through the church service, trying to support Mum, and we then follow the coffin to the ferry. Dad has requested he be cremated, and the nearest facility is in Greenock, across the Clyde, so we cross the water and then follow the cortege to the crematorium. It's a long and tiring day for everyone, and we all travel back to Sandbank in silence, each immersed in their own thoughts and memories.

I am able to stay and support Mum for a week in Sandbank, thanks to my Glasgow friends, and then she returns with me to Glasgow to stay until she feels ready to return home and live alone.

Surviving and Thriving

Chapter Fourteen

Resolving our Routines

With Ngozi now aged four, it is time to consider mainstream school enrolment for her, so I research the local schools. I realise that if I sell our current flat and move to a different part of the city we will be in the catchment area of a school which has an excellent reputation. It is the primary school adjoining the local teacher training college where I originally trained. This looks like a sensible option and so I go house hunting once more. I put my one-bedroom flat on the market and I am pleasantly surprised at its valuation. This is not just on account of the improved upgrade I have achieved within the flat, but because house prices are rising significantly across the board. I do my research and locate a ground floor flat in an upmarket area within the part of the city where I would like to be based. There is the added attraction of a play park at the end of the street which Ngozi will be able to use. The fact that the street is a cul-de-sac is a safety benefit, so I put in an offer and impatiently await the outcome. When I hear that I am outbid I am quite tearful. The process of purchasing my original flat had been so smooth and uncomplicated that I was expecting this purchase to be the same. Friends console me with the suggestion that the park would not have been a long-term facility for Ngozi. So I have to start the process again.

The next flat I'm interested in is also on the ground level. This time I am looking at a substantial red sandstone building. The flat has three bedrooms and a small front garden as well as a large basement area below the kitchen. The basement gives access to a back garden which is the sole preserve of the owner of this particular flat. I'm looking at the potential for letting one of the rooms within this flat where I will actually be living and thus be in a good position to monitor what goes on. I make an offer on the property and pray for a positive outcome. If this comes to fruition it will allow me to enrol Ngozi in a good primary school and will be a long term home for us, with extra space for visitors or lodgers. I'm really praying hard for this to become a reality. I have received so many answers to so many prayers over my many dilemmas in reaching this point in my life, so I pray in the belief that God will provide the appropriate answers to my requests.

The news finally arrives, and it's a positive outcome. *Thank you, Lord!* Things are finally falling into place for me as a single parent. A home, a car, the school I want for Ngozi, new options for employment and really good friends from my church connection. The decoration process begins all over again, but as I have minimal house contents, I can occupy some rooms, decorate empty rooms and then switch around as necessary. I had learned much from watching my brothers decorate the previous flat. Mum comes to visit, stays for a while and is obviously amazed at how I have managed to get my life together. She is also pleased that I am living in a relatively leafy part of town with a small garden area just waiting for development. She knows my "green fingers" will not be idle for long.

I secure a teaching post in Paisley, working in the remedial department of Camphill Secondary School. The pupils' age range is 12 to 15, and they are all in need of specialised support for a variety of reasons. The teaching is highly individualised and I am well qualified to provide it. This job means a journey from the city, through the Clyde tunnel and ten miles further on into Paisley. Ngozi has one more year before officially starting at Jordanhill Primary School, so I enrol her in a local pre-school nursery, where I can drop her off en route to my job, and collect her on my return. This seems a happy solution and my spirits are high as this routine falls into place. However, it seems that nothing in my life is guaranteed to run smoothly! A few weeks in and Ngozi is ill with German measles. I take time off school and others members of staff cover my teaching duties. Soon I'm back at school and it's not long before the next crisis arrives. Ngozi's nursery is affected by dysentery, and although Ngozi is diagnosed as clear, the nursery is closed for a period of time so that deep cleaning can be undertaken. I require time off again from my teaching duties. I am fast becoming the subject of much resentment among colleagues as there are also the inevitable bouts of colds and flu to deal with over the winter. Just short of two years at the school, and after six absences on parental responsibility grounds, I decided to call it a day and look for work closer to home.

This time I decided to focus on my educational psychology qualifications. An opportunity comes along to work as one of a team at Fern Tower clinic which is a facility where work with school-refusing children is undertaken. During school hours I will be working in a classroom style environment with a small number of children of secondary school age. However, I am also required to offer therapeutic family support once a week in the evening to the parents and their child. I approach a couple who are friends in the church who live close to Ngozi's school and seek their help in finding a local child minder to cover my evening stint at the clinic. The couple are long term residents in the area and I presume they may have the kind of information I need about available childminders. They agree to think about my request and when they finally come back to me I am completely overwhelmed. My friends make an offer that I can't refuse.

Ngozi and I have been frequent visitors to their home, and they have four children. Their youngest, Alison, is a year older than Ngozi, and the girls are already good friends. On the evenings when I work at the clinic, Ngozi will go home from school with Alison, stay for her evening meal, and will be there for me to collect at bed-time. No money will change hands! And so life as a single parent begins again to feel more stable and settled.

Back at the clinic: why are children refusing to go to school? They often use excuses relating to health: sore tummies, sore heads, feeling sick etc. etc. etc. but when the issues are more closely examined, it transpires that sometimes other children are bullying them, or perhaps they are failing to understand new knowledge, or the transfer from a small primary school to a large secondary school has an overwhelming impact and they just cannot find the emotional courage to enter the school gates. Once more I love my employment on two counts. Firstly, there are no classroom behavioural disturbances, and secondly, I can try to resolve the youngsters' deep-seated problems. I'm used to problem solving. It's been the story of my life in many ways, and generally, I have been adept at responding positively.

As the summer holidays approach, I decide to discuss a project with the young people. They are enthusiastic at my suggestion of remaining together as a group and doing fun things during their holidays. I make arrangements through the education department for access to a local community centre, and a mid-day meal for our project group. Plans are progressing well and anticipation is building, when, with no warning or reason given, the department pulls out and cancels the plans. The young people are angry and desperately disappointed, but there is nothing I can do to salvage the situation. So we bid each other farewell at the end of the term and express good wishes for whatever the summer break now holds for us all.

Chapter Fifteen

A Final Adventure

For me, the holiday period now feels empty. Ngozi was so looking forward to being with me during the project and was gutted that she could no longer mix with "the big boys and girls". *How can I redeem this situation?* I make a suggestion,

"Let's go on a camping holiday to Mull and look for Spanish gold. A big ship sank in Tobermory Bay and it had lots of gold on board. Maybe if we scour the beach we will be lucky and find some."

This suggestion is met with squeals of delight and so the matter is settled. We pack our car with all the necessities: a tent, sleeping bags, a gas camping stove and all the other paraphernalia we will require and set off.

We drive north into the countryside, following along the banks of Loch Lomond, singing the famous folk songs associated with the loch, and admiring the changing views as we journey. Then we strike west heading for the sea-side town of Oban.

I check the schedules for car ferries as that will be the next stage of our journey: leaving the mainland behind, heading west to the Isle of Mull. This is not a first for me. I have often before driven a car onto a ferry, and once safely on board, we go up on deck to enjoy the sea air and try to spot dolphins, sharks or whales, as all are frequent visitors to Scotland's west coast.

Forty minutes later we leave the ferry and drive off to look for a suitable camp site.

"When can we look for gold?" asks Ngozi, and I realise that unless we do that first there will be no rest for me. So we drive to Tobermory, the small town with the famous cat, and the brightly painted houses along the sea front.

"Look, Mummy, the houses are just like on television," comes the excited voice from the back seat of the car.

.She is right. The children's TV programme "Balamory" uses these houses as a backdrop, so it is easy to make the connection. There is also a photographer in the town who captured a local stray cat on film in various situations and added humorous captions to his photos. His collection was later published in book form as "The Tobermory Cat" and it quickly became a best seller. So much so that visitors to Tobermory are often seen looking for the cat. *We* manage to spot him, asleep in the sunny window of the youth hostel. Then it is a trip to the beach to look for our Spanish gold. We scour the beach, eyes down, turning over lots of stones of varying colours; white quartz, pink sandstone, black haematite and green serpentine, but no gold, not even any pyrites.

"Mummy, you told me we would find gold here, but there's none." pouts a disappointed Ngozi.

"Lots of people look for it and it's hard to spot, but look at all the lovely coloured stones we have found to take home."

A promise to return the following day alleviates the disappointment and we head back to the car to go and find a camping site. So we drive onwards and soon discover a quiet sandy bay with some rough ground nearby which provides the perfect site for our tent. As I unload the car I ask Ngozi to help me.

"You know how to hold the pole for me and I can fix the guy ropes," I suggest.

But as I unfold the tent and turn round to pass her the pole, there is no Ngozi to be seen. Where is she? In the car? At the other side of the car? NOOO. Then where? I glance towards the beach just in time to see her disappearing around a headland. Running in panic, stumbling over the grass and then hampered by soft dry deep sand I fear the worst. Rounding the headland I spot her. Relief floods my body. She is alone. I catch up with her and she is taken aback at my angry comments.

"What are you doing?" I yell. "I asked you for help and you ran away without telling me!" I was still shouting I was so upset.

"Mummy," she whimpers, "I'm only looking for crabs in the rock pools."

"You know you must not go away without telling me." I snap, and then let the matter rest.

As darkness descends we sit at the door of the tent and watch an amazing sunset; pinks and reds streaking across the sky, merging into a soft orange glow as the sun finally dips below the horizon. We settle into our sleeping bags. Wakening to another lovely morning I find Ngozi is far from well. She is finding it extremely difficult to breathe. What am I to do in this situation? Obviously, she needs medical attention, and quickly, so we abandon our camping site and return post haste to Tobermory. Fortunately, we secure an early appointment at the local surgery. The doctor examines Ngozi and then asks for privacy with me and a nurse takes my daughter aside.

"What are you thinking of, camping without checking pollen count forecasts? Didn't you see how high they were expected to be? Are you stupid?" He demands of me.

I remain silent under this totally unexpected onslaught.

"Unless you promise to forget about this camping nonsense, and sleep under a proper roof tonight, there will be no prescription!" he barks at me.

What am I to do? With no real choice available, I make the promise and we leave the surgery with a prescription for an inhaler to counteract what the doctor has diagnosed as a severe allergic rhinitis attack. We look in the main street for the local chemist and collect the prescribed inhaler. I sit in the car, my head in my hands. What a disaster! Abandon our adventure? For a second time, our holiday plans have been thwarted, this time courtesy of the doctor. What choice do I have? Will we simply return ignominiously to Glasgow, and leave the Spanish gold behind? *No chance*!! Somehow I *will* find an adventure. Suddenly I spot a B&B sign. Maybe we can stay in Tobermory after all and look for our gold. I knock the door, but no vacancies. Next B&B, same answer. Is third time going to be lucky perhaps? But no, it is the same negative answer. *Is this because Ngozi is a mixed race child?* I recall a famous Irish authoress who wrote, "Prejudices are the chains forged by ignorance to keep men apart".

For sure, I'm no longer enjoying this so-called adventure; there are so many situations I can't resolve.

Returning to our camping site, with Ngozi sniffing, miserable and disappointed, we start to dismantle the tent and store all our gear in the car boot. As we pack, I am still trying to find an answer to "having an adventure". Then from somewhere in the dim and distant past, I hear my father's voice talking about an abbey with a Christian community on the Isle of Iona. Is this a viable choice? Or will it just be a third disaster? I decide to risk it and make a telephone call. There is indeed accommodation, and this seems a possible way of salvaging some semblance of adventure. So we drive to Fionnphort (Gaelic), park the car and take the small ferry across a narrow stretch of water to Iona.

I am full of trepidation. Is this the right choice to make? Living in a community situation will be a new experience for us. Tensions remain for me. *Who else will be there? Will it be a Bible-thumping group? Do they have an ecumenical outlook? Would they condemn me for my camping adventure with young Ngozi?* So many anxious thoughts about the unknown.

When we arrive at the Abbey we find a group of German pastors holding a conference. They have come to Iona to learn about the social justice work in which the community is involved. With no hesitation, they simply absorb us into their midst. I join them during their discussions and we are invited to go with them on their boat trip to Fingal's Cave on Staffa. Ultimately we enjoy many positive experiences.

Ngozi is fascinated by the findings of the resident archaeologist—the bones man—as she calls him. I spend time in the library absorbing information about ancient Celtic art and culture. We learn a lot about the social justice work of the community, we explore the island and worship daily in the Abbey Church., What had been a fearful, apprehensive, anxious choice, is now giving me much food for thought. Is this how my Glasgow teenagers feel about school as they, in turn, face so many unknowns? I now had some relevant experiences around major life changes and difficult emotional choices to share with them, along with increased empathy for their individual situations.

We never did find the gold on the shoreline, but our contact with the Iona community turned out to be gold of another sort by providing friends, support, employment and many other opportunities.

Surviving and Thriving

Epilogue

So where does all this now leave me now? As I reflect on my life experiences during the years between the sixties and the seventies, I can say with assurance that God's hand was surely on me. It takes a degree of resilience and persistence to survive and thrive as I have done, but the possibility is always there. So, who am I now? I believe myself to be a strong woman, crafted by unusual circumstances; instead of succumbing to events around me, I have taken fairly decisive action and come through time after time. Was I never afraid? Of course I was, sometimes even terrified. Many times it would have been easier to "go with the flow", but by rising to the challenges I was able to overcome them. It reflects the message in the well-known book titled "Face the Fear and Do It Anyway" by Susan Jeffers. How true that has been for me. I don't think life in the quiet village of Sandbank, in an ordinary family could possibly have made me who I am today. Experiencing and reacting to hard, unexpected and difficult circumstances has been the mould that fashioned me. Maybe my parents were right in some ways with their advice, and by making the mistake of ignoring it, so much suffering came my way, but in the end, it seems to have worked out all right.

Life is, of course, a continuum; and life has been good to me and Ngozi. For me, a succession of summer holidays spent on Iona working at the youth camp there led to employment in Edinburgh, as I was "head-hunted" to run a working girls' residential home for nine girls who had previously been in trouble with the law. That was a tough one. Being a live-in warden with Ngozi alongside me led to threats from one of the more aggressive girls regarding Ngozi's safety as she travelled by bus to and from school. Unfortunately, the home was subsequently closed down so my employment there ceased. Contacts with Edinburgh church friends led us to move to the then new town of Livingston where I opted for self-employment. That was a scary choice at the time but served us well. I did some medical research for the University of Newcastle, some home tutoring, fostering, and work as an education liaison officer. My work experience and skill set was adaptable and growing. A few years later in the eighties, another geographical move took us to the highlands of Scotland, where I became the joint proprietor of a small tourism-focussed business, producing knitwear with Celtic designs. These intricate patterns were an off-shoot of time spent in the library on Iona. While living and working in Edinburgh

I had initiated divorce proceedings against Sennen in 1975, and as it was uncontested I felt a freedom to move on in my relationships. At the time I was attending a Pentecostal church and it was here I met Ron, my present husband, and the co-owner of our highland-based business. We named the business Gander Crafts as the gander was the Celtic symbol for the Holy Spirit. We still live in the highlands and have been married now for over thirty years.

And what of Ngozi? Naturally, she had many questions about her father. I answered her honestly, but with discretion, about anything she wanted to know—even the bad times. She sometimes sought to be told she was an adopted child, which I suspect was in response to others posing that question to her. As she grew older she spoke often of wanting to return to Nigeria and seek out her father. My response to this was that I would support her, but that I would not go back. When she reached her mid-teens I investigated the possibility of her staying with known missionaries to support her search, as I felt this would be a safe option in what I saw to be an increasingly corrupt country where she would be so innocent. Eventually, however, the desire on her part waned and she never made the journey. However, her interest in Nigerian affairs continued, and as an adult, she was excited to discover via the internet that someone was searching for her. In responding, she discovered that the reason she was being sought was that her father had died in 2000, and as the eldest child amongst several—all girls—she was the inheritor of a variety of investment assets. This led to a visit from the next eldest daughter to this country and contact between them. It went well for a little while, but eventually, the friendship faded and Ngozi has settled into life in this country with some of her questions and desires resolved and others still seeking closure. Her father's assets were never realised by her, and she is content to leave it like that.

Friends tell me that when they have a problem, they think of my experiences, and that helps them to see their own difficulties from a totally different perspective. I'm glad if my story and struggles can help others in their circumstances. Courage, determination and a strong faith have been my building blocks.

I feel proud of my achievements, particularly how I flourished and blossomed as a single parent, and succeeded in remaining financially independent. It has not always been easy. However, I have been able to pull through all the intense and multifarious problems I faced with sometimes unexpected, but always welcome support from family, church, friends, and indeed strangers. So to others facing what can seem like unsurmountable dilemmas, I say, "Be bold, tenacious and courageous. I did it and you can do it too."

"Happiness consists not in having much, but in being content with little."

(Countess of Blessington 1789 – 1894)

Printed in September 2019
by Rotomail Italia S.p.A., Vignate (MI) - Italy